THE POEMS
AND PROSE POEMS OF
CHARLES BAUDELAIRE

WITH AN INTRODUCTORY PREFACE BY
JAMES HUNEKER

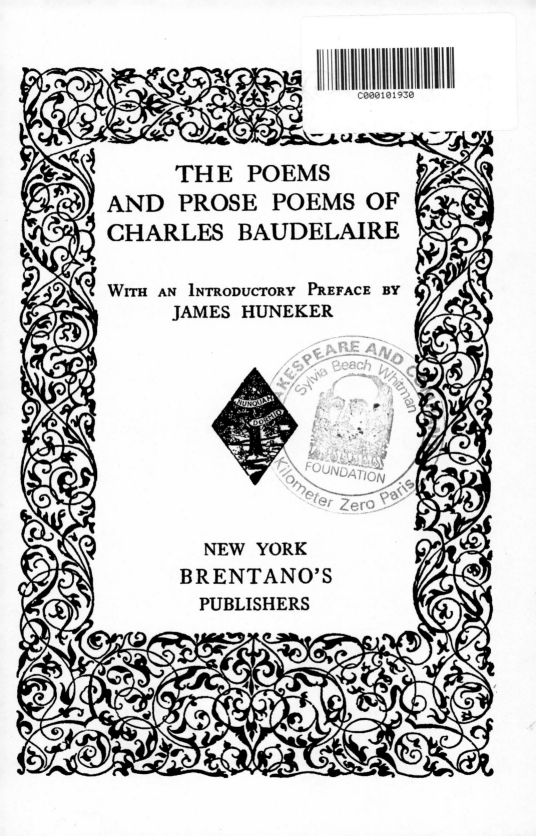

NEW YORK
BRENTANO'S
PUBLISHERS

PRINTED IN THE UNITED STATES OF AMERICA
THE PLIMPTON PRESS · NORWOOD · MASS

CONTENTS.

CONTENTS.

CONTENTS.

CHARLES BAUDELAIRE.

By JAMES HUNEKER.

I

FOR the sentimental no greater foe exists than the iconoclast who dissipates literary legends. And he is abroad nowadays. Those golden times when they gossiped of De Quincey's enormous opium consumption, of the gin absorbed by gentle Charles Lamb, of Coleridge's dark ways, Byron's escapades, and Shelley's atheism — alas! into what faded limbo have they vanished. Poe, too, whom we saw in fancy reeling from Richmond to Baltimore, Baltimore to Philadelphia, Philadelphia to New York. Those familiar fascinating anecdotes have gone the way of all such jerry-built spooks. We now know Poe to have been a man suffering at the time of his death from cerebral lesion, a man who drank at intervals and little. Dr. Guerrier of Paris has exploded a darling superstition about De Quincey's opium-eating. He has demonstrated that no man could have lived so long — De Quincey was nearly seventy-five at his death — and worked so hard, if he had consumed twelve thousand drops of laudanum as often as he said he did. Furthermore, the English essayist's description of the drug's effects is inexact. He was seldom sleepy — a sure sign, asserts Dr. Guerrier, that he was not altogether enslaved by the drug habit. Sprightly in old age, his powers of labour were prolonged until past three-score and ten. His imagination needed little opium to produce the famous Confessions. Even Gautier's revolutionary red waistcoat worn at the première of Hernani was, according to Gautier, a pink doublet. And Rousseau has been whitewashed. So they are disappearing, those literary legends, until, disheartened, we cry out: Spare us our dear, old-fashioned, disreputable men of genius!

But the legend of Charles Baudelaire is seemingly indestructible. This French poet has suffered more from the friendly malignant biographer and chroniclers than did Poe. Who shall keep the curs out of the cemetery? asked Baudelaire after he had read Griswold on Poe. A few years later his own cemetery was invaded and the world was put into possession of the Baudelaire legend; that legend of the atrabilious, irritable poet, dandy, maniac, his hair dyed green, spouting blasphemies; that grim, despairing image of a diabolic, a libertine, saint, and drunkard. Maxime du Camp was much to blame for the promulgation of these tales — witness his Souvenirs littéraires. However, it may be confessed that part of the Baudelaire legend was created by Charles Baudelaire. In the history of literature it is difficult to parallel such a deliberate piece of self-stultification. Not Villon, who preceded him, not Verlaine, who imitated him, drew for the astonishment or disedification of the world a like unflattering portrait. Mystifier as he was, he must have suffered at times from acute cortical irritation. And, notwithstanding his desperate effort to realize Poe's idea, he only proved Poe correct, who had said that no man can bare his heart quite naked; there always will be something held back, something false ostentatiously thrust forward. The grimace, the attitude, the pomp of rhetoric are so many buffers between the soul of man and the sharp reality of published confessions. Baudelaire was no more exception to this rule than St. Augustine, Bunyan, Rousseau, or Huysmans; though he was as frank as any of them, as we may see in the printed diary, Mon cœur mis à nu (Posthumous Works, Société du Mercure de France); and in the Journal, Fusées, Letters, and other fragments exhumed by devoted Baudelarians.

To smash legends, Eugène Crépet's biographical study, first printed in 1887, has been republished with new notes by his son, Jacques Crépet. This is an exceedingly valuable contribution to Baudelaire lore; a dispassionate life, however, has yet to be written, a noble task for some young poet who will disentangle the conflicting lies originated by Baudelaire — that tragic comedian — from the truth and thus save him from himself. The Crépet volume is really but a series of notes; there are some letters addressed to the poet by the distinguished men of his day, supplementing the rather disappointing volume of Letters, 1841–1866, published in 1908. There are also documents in the legal prosecution of Baudelaire, with memories of him by Charles Asselineau, Léon Cladel, Camille Lemonnier, and others.

In November, 1850, Maxime du Camp and

CHARLES BAUDELAIRE.

Gustave Flaubert found themselves at the French Ambassador's, Constantinople. The two friends had taken a trip in the Orient which later bore fruit in Salammbô. General Aupick, the representative of the French Government, cordially the young men received; they were presented to his wife, Madame Aupick. She was the mother of Charles Baudelaire, and inquired rather anxiously of Du Camp: "My son has talent, has he not?" Unhappy because her second marriage, a brilliant one, had set her son against her, the poor woman welcomed from such a source confirmation of her eccentric boy's gifts. Du Camp tells the much-discussed story of a quarrel between the youthful Charles and his stepfather, a quarrel that began at table. There were guests present. After some words Charles bounded at the General's throat and sought to strangle him. He was promptly boxed on the ears and succumbed to a nervous spasm. A delightful anecdote, one that fills with joy psychiatrists in search of a theory of genius and degeneration. Charles was given some money and put on board a ship sailing to East India. He became a cattle-dealer in the British army, and returned to France years afterward with a Vénus noire, to whom he addressed extravagant poems! All this according to Du Camp. Here is another tale, a comical one. Baudelaire visited Du Camp in Paris, and his hair was violently green. Du Camp said nothing. Angered by this indifference, Baudelaire asked: "You find nothing abnormal about me?" "No," was the answer. "But my hair — it is green!" "That is not singular, mon cher Baudelaire; every one has hair more or less green in Paris." Disappointed in not creating a sensation, Baudelaire went to a café, gulped down two large bottles of Burgundy, and asked the waiter to remove the water, as water was a disagreeable sight; then he went away in a rage. It is a pity to doubt this green hair legend; presently a man of genius will not be able to enjoy an epileptic fit in peace — as does a banker or a beggar. We are told that St. Paul, Mahomet, Handel, Napoleon, Flaubert, Dostoievsky were epileptoids; yet we do not encounter men of this rare kind among the inmates of asylums. Even Baudelaire had his sane moments.

The joke of the green hair has been disposed of by Crépet. Baudelaire's hair thinning after an illness, he had his head shaved and painted with salve of a green hue, hoping thereby to escape baldness. At the time when he had embarked for Calcutta (May, 1841), he was not seventeen, but twenty years of age. Du Camp said he was seventeen when he attacked General Aupick. The dinner could not have taken place at Lyons because the Aupick family had left that city six years before the date given by Du Camp. Charles was provided with five thousand francs for his expenses, instead of twenty — Du Camp's version — and he never was a beef-drover in the British army, for a good reason — he never reached India. Instead, he disembarked at the Isle of Bourbon, and after a short stay suffered from homesickness and returned to France, after being absent about ten months. But, like Flaubert, on his return home Baudelaire was seized with the nostalgia of the East; over there he had yearned for Paris. Jules Claretie recalls Baudelaire saying to him with a grimace: " I love Wagner; but the music I prefer is that of a cat hung up by his tail outside of a window, and trying to stick to the panes of glass with its claws. There is an odd grating on the glass which I find at the same time strange, irritating, and singularly harmonious." Is it necessary to add that Baudelaire, notorious in Paris for his love of cats, dedicating poems to cats, would never have perpetrated such revolting cruelty?

Another misconception, a critical one, is the case of Poe and Baudelaire. The young Frenchman first became infatuated with Poe's writings in 1846 or 1847 — he gave these two dates, though several stories of Poe had been translated into French as early as 1841 or 1842; L'Orang-Outang was the first, which we know as The Murders in the Rue Morgue; Madame Meunier also adapted several Poe stories for the reviews. Baudelaire's labours as a translator lasted over ten years. That he assimilated Poe, that he idolized Poe, is a commonplace of literary gossip. But that Poe had overwhelming influence in the formation of his poetic genius is not the truth. Yet we find such an acute critic as the late Edmund Clarence Stedman writing, "Poe's chief influence upon Baudelaire's own production relates to poetry." It is precisely the reverse. Poe's influence affected Baudelaire's prose, notably in the disjointed confessions, Mon cœur mis à nu, which vaguely recall the American writer's Marginalia. The bulk in the poetry in Les Fleurs du Mal was written before Baudelaire had read Poe, though not published in book form until 1857. But in 1855 some of the poems saw the light in the Revue des deux Mondes, while many of them had been put forth a decade or fifteen years before as fugitive verse in various magazines. Stedman was not the first to make this mistake. In Bayard Taylor's The Echo Club we find on page 24 this criticism: " There was a congenital twist about Poe . . . Baudelaire and Swinburne after him have been trying to surpass him by increasing the dose; but his muse is the natural Pythia inheriting her convulsions, while they eat all sorts of insane roots to produce theirs." This must have been written about 1872, and after reading it one would fancy that Poe and Baudelaire were rhapsodic wrigglers on the poetic tripod, whereas their poetry is often reserved, even glacial. Baudelaire, like Poe, sometimes " built his nests with the birds of Night," and that was enough to condemn the work of both men by critics of the didactic school.

Once, when Baudelaire heard that an Ameri-

CHARLES BAUDELAIRE.

can man of letters (?) was in Paris, he secured an introduction and called on him. Eagerly inquiring after Poe, he learned that he was not considered a genteel person in America, Baudelaire withdrew, muttering maledictions. Enthusiastic poet! Charming literary person! Yet the American, whoever he was, represented public opinion at the time. To-day criticisms of Poe are vitiated by the desire to make him an angel. It is to be doubted whether without his barren environment and hard fortunes we should have had Poe at all. He had to dig down deep into the pit of his personality to reach the central core of his music. But every ardent young soul entering "literature" begins by a vindication of Poe's character. Poe was a man, and he is now a classic. He was a half-charlatan as was Baudelaire. In both the sublime and the sickly were never far asunder. The pair loved to mystify, to play pranks on their contemporaries. Both were implacable pessimists. Both were educated in affluence, and both had to face unprepared the hardships of life. The hastiest comparison of their poetic work will show that their only common ideal was the worship of an exotic beauty. Their

CHARLES BAUDELAIRE.

artistic methods of expression were totally dis-
similar. Baudelaire, like Poe, had a harp-like
temperament which vibrated in the presence of
strange subjects. Above all, he was obsessed
by sex. Women, as angel of destruction, is the
keynote of his poems. Poe was almost sexless.
His aerial creatures never footed the dusty
highways of the world. His lovely lines,
" Helen, thy beauty is to me," could never have
been written by Baudelaire; while Poe would
never have pardoned the " fulgurant " gran-
deur, the Beethoven-like harmonies, the Dan-
tesque horrors of that " deep wide music of
lost souls" in " Femmes Damnées " :

"Descendes, descendes, lamentable victimes."

Or this, which might serve as a text for one
of John Martin's vast sinister mezzotints:

J'ai vu parfois au fond d'un théâtre banal
Qu'enflammait l'orchestre sonore,
Une fée allumer dans un ciel infernal
Une miraculeuse aurore;

J'ai vu parfois au fond d'un théâtre banal
Un être, qui n'était que lumière, or et gaze,

CHARLES BAUDELAIRE.

Terrasser l'énorme Satan;
Mais mon cœur que jamais ne visite l'extase,
Est un théâtre où l'on attend
Toujours, toujours en vain l'Etre aux ailes de gaze.

George Saintsbury thus sums up the differences between Poe and Baudelaire: "Both authors — Poe and De Quincey — fell short of Baudelaire himself as regards depth and fulness of passion, but both have a superficial likeness to him in eccentricity of temperament and affection for a certain peculiar mixture of grotesque and horror." Poe is without passion, except a passion for the macabre; what Huysmans calls "The October of the sensations"; whereas, there is a gulf of despair and terror and humanity in Baudelaire, which shakes your nerves, yet stimulates the imagination. However, profounder as a poet, he was no match for Poe in what might be termed intellectual prestidigitation. The mathematical Poe, the Poe of the ingenious detective tales, tales extraordinary, the Poe of the swift flights into the cosmic blue, the Poe the prophet and mystic — in these the American was more versatile than his French translator. That Baudelaire said, "Evil be thou my good," is doubtless true. He proved all things and found them vanity. He is the poet of original sin, a worshipper of Satan for the sake of paradox; his Litanies to Satan ring childish to us — in his heart he was a believer. His was " an infinite reverse aspiration," and mixed up with his pose was a disgust for vice, for life itself. He was the last of the Romanticists; Sainte-Beuve called him the Kamchatka of Romanticism; its remotest hyperborean peak. Romanticism is dead to-day, as dead as Naturalism; but Baudelaire is alive, and read. His glistening phosphorescent trail is over French poetry and he is the begetter of a school: — Verlaine, Villiers de l'Isle Adam, Carducci, Arthur Rimbaud, Jules Laforgue, Gabriel D'Annunzio, Aubrey Beardsley, Verhaeren, and many of the youthful crew. He affected Swinburne, and in Huysmans, who was not a poet, his splenetic spirit lives. Baudelaire's motto might be the obverse of Browning's lines: " The Devil is in heaven. All's wrong with the world."

When Goethe said of Hugo and the Romanticists that they came from Chateaubriand, he should have substituted the name of Rousseau — " Romanticism, it is Rousseau," exclaims Pierre Lasserre. But there is more of Byron and Petrus Borel — a forgotten half-mad poet — in Baudelaire; though, for a brief period, in 1848, he became a Rousseau reactionary, sported the workingman's blouse, cut his hair, shouldered a musket, went to the barricades, wrote inflammatory editorials calling the proletarian " Brother!" (oh, Baudelaire!) and, as the Goncourts recorded in their diary, had the head of a maniac. How seriously we may take this swing of the pendulum is to be noted in a speech of the poet's at the time of the Revolution: " Come," he said, " let us go shoot General Aupick!" It was his stepfather that he thought of, not the eternal principles of Liberty. This may be a false anecdote; many such were foisted upon Baudelaire. For example, his exclamations at cafés or in public places, such as: " Have you ever eaten a baby? I find it pleasing to the palate!" or, " The night I killed my father!" Naturally, people stared and Baudelaire was happy — he had startled a bourgeois. The cannibalistic idea he may have borrowed from Swift's amusing pamphlet, for this French poet knew English literature.

CHARLES BAUDELAIRE.

Gautier compares the poems to a certain tale of Hawthorne's in which there is a garden of poisoned flowers. But Hawthorne worked in his laboratory of evil wearing mask and gloves; he never descended into the mud and sin of the street. Baudelaire ruined his health, smudged his soul, yet remained withal, as Anatole France says, "a divine poet." How childish, yet how touching is his resolution — he wrote in his diary of prayer's dynamic force — when he was penniless, in debt, threatened with imprisonment, sick, nauseated with sin: "To make every morning my prayer to God, the reservoir of all force, and all justice; to my father, to Mariette, and to Poe as intercessors." (Evidently, Maurice Barrès encountered here his theory of Intercessors.) Baudelaire loved the memory of his father as much as Stendhal hated his own. He became reconciled with his mother after the death of General Aupick, in 1857. He felt in 1862 that his own intellectual eclipse was approaching, for he wrote: "I have cultivated my hysteria with joy and terror. To-day imbecility's wing fanned me as it passed." The sense of the vertiginous gulf was abiding with him; read his poem, "Pascal avait son gouffre."

CHARLES BAUDELAIRE.

In preferring the Baudelaire translations of Poe to the original — and they give the impression of being original works — Stedman agreed with Asselineau that the French is more concise than the English. The prose of Poe and Baudelaire is clear, sober, rhythmic; Baudelaire's is more lapidary, finer in contour, richer coloured, more supple, though without the "honey and tiger's blood" of Barbey d'Aurevilly. Baudelaire's soul was patiently built up as a fabulous bird might build its nest — bits of straw, the sobbing of women, clay, cascades of black stars, rags, leaves, rotten wood, corroding dreams, a spray of roses, a sparkle of pebble, a gleam of blue sky, arabesques of incense and verdigris, despairing hearts and music and the abomination of desolation, for its ground-tones. But this soul-nest is also a cemetery of the seven sorrows. He loves the clouds . . . les nuages . . . là bas. . . . It was là bas with him even in the tortures of his wretched love-life. Corruption and death were ever floating in his consciousness. He was like Flaubert, who saw everywhere the hidden skeleton. Félicien Rops has best interpreted Baudelaire; the etcher and poet were closely knit spirits.

CHARLES BAUDELAIRE.

Rodin, too, is a Baudelarian.. If there could be such an anomaly as a native wood-note wildly evil, it would be the lyric and astringent voice of this poet. His sensibility was both catholic and morbid, though he could be frigid in the face of the most disconcerting misfortunes. He was a man for whom the invisible word existed; if Gautier was pagan, Baudelaire was a strayed spirit from mediæval days. The spirit rules, and, as Paul Bourget said, " he saw God." A Manichean in his worship of evil, he nevertheless abased his soul: " Oh! Lord God! Give me the force and courage to contemplate my heart and my body without disgust," he prays: but as some one remarked to Rochefoucauld, " Where you end, Christianity begins."

Baudelaire built his ivory tower on the borders of a poetic Maremma, which every miasma of the spirit pervaded, every marsh-light and glow-worm inhabited. Like Wagner, Baudelaire painted in his sultry music the profundities of abysms, the vastness of space. He painted, too, the great nocturnal silences of the soul.

Pacem summum tenent! He never reached

peace on the heights. Let us admit that souls of his kind are encased in sick frames; their steel is too shrewd for the scabbard; yet the enigma for us is none the less unfathomable. Existence for such natures is a sort of muffled delirium. To affiliate him with Poe, De Quincey, Hoffman, James Thomson, Coleridge, and the rest of the sombre choir does not explain him; he is, perhaps, nearer Donne and Villon than any of the others — strains of the metaphysical and sinister and supersubtle are to be discovered in him. The disharmony of brain and body, the spiritual bilocation, are only too easy to diagnose; but the remedy? Hypocrite lecteur — mon semblable — mon frère! When the subtlety, force, grandeur, of his poetic production be considered, together with its disquieting, nervous, vibrating qualities, it is not surprising that Victor Hugo wrote to the poet: "You invest the heaven of art with we know not what deadly rays; you create a new shudder." Hugo might have said that he turned Art into an Inferno. Baudelaire is the evil archangel of poetry. In his heaven of fire, glass and ebony he is the blazing Lucifer. "A glorious devil, large in heart and brain, that did love beauty only . . ." once sang Tennyson, though not of the Frenchman.

II

As long ago as 1869, and in our " barbarous gas-lit country," as Baudelaire named the land of Poe, an unsigned review appeared in which this poet was described as " unique and as interesting as Hamlet. He is that rare and unknown being, a genuine poet — a poet in the midst of things that have disordered his spirit — a poet excessively developed in his taste for and by beauty . . . very responsive to the ideal, very greedy of sensation." A better description of Baudelaire does not exist. The Hamlet-motive, particularly, is one that sounded throughout the disordered symphony of the poet's life.

He was, later, revealed — also reviled — to American readers by Henry James, who completely missed his significance. This was in 1878, when appeared the first edition of French Poets and Novelists. Previous to that there had been some desultory discussion, a few essays in the magazines, and in 1875 a sympathetic paper by Professor James Albert Harrison of the University of Virginia. He denounced the Frenchman for his reprehensible taste, though he did not mention his beautiful verse nor his originality in the matter of criticism. Baudelaire, in his eyes, was not only immoral, but he had, with the approbation of Sainte-Beuve, introduced Poe as a great man to the French nation. (See Baudelaire's letter to Sainte-Beuve in the newly published Letters, 1841–1866.) Perhaps " Mr. Dick Minim " and his projected Academy of Criticism might make clear these devious problems.

The Etudes Critiques of Edmond Schérer were collected in 1863. In them we find this unhappy, uncritical judgment: " Baudelaire, lui, n'a rien, ni le cœur, ni l'esprit, ni l'idée, ni le mot, ni la raison, ni la fantaisie, ni la verve, ni même la facture . . . son unique titre c'est d'avoir contribué à créer l'esthétique de la débauche." It is not our intention to dilate upon the injustice of this criticism. It is Baudelaire the critic of æsthetics in whom we are interested. Yet I cannot forbear saying that if all the negations of Schérer had been transformed into affirmations, only justice would have been accorded Baudelaire, who was not alone a poet, the most original of his century, but also a critic of the first rank, one who welcomed Richard Wagner when Paris hooted him and his fellow composer, Hector Berlioz, played the rôle of the envious; one who fought for Edouard Manet, Leconte de Lisle, Gustave Flaubert, Eugène Delacroix; fought with pen for the modern etchers, illustrators, Meryon, Daumier, Félicien Rops, Gavarni, and Constantin Guys. He literally identified himself with De Quincey and Poe, translating them so wonderfully well that some unpatriotic persons like the French better than the originals. So much was Baudelaire absorbed in Poe that a writer of his times asserted that the translator would meet the same fate as the American poet. A singular, vigorous spirit is Baudelaire's, whose poetry with its "icy ecstasy" is profound and harmonious, whose criticism is penetrated by a catholic quality, who anticipated modern critics in his abhorrence of schools and environments, preferring to isolate the man and uniquely study him. He would have subscribed to Swinburne's generous pronouncement: " I have never been able to see what should attract man to the profession of criticism but the noble pleasure of praising." The Frenchman has said that it would be impossible for a critic to become a poet; and it is impossible for a poet not to contain a critic.

Théophile Gautier's study prefixed to the definitive edition of Les Fleurs du Mal is not only the most sympathetic exposition of Baudelaire as man and genius, but it is also the high-water mark of Gautier's gifts as a critical essayist. We learn therein how the young Charles, an incorrigible dandy, came to visit Hôtel Pimodan about 1844. In this Hôtel Pimodan a dilettante, Ferdinand Boissard, held high revel. His fantastically decorated apartments were frequented by the painters, poets, sculptors, romancers, of the day — that is, carefully selected ones such as Liszt, George Sand, Mérimée, and others whose verve or genius gave them the privilege of saying Open Sesame! to this cave of forty Supermen. Balzac has in his Peau de Chagrin pictured the same sort of scenes which were supposed to occur weekly at the Pimodan. Gautier eloquently describes the meeting of these kindred artistic souls, where the beautiful Jewess, Maryx, who had posed for Ary Scheffer's

CHARLES BAUDELAIRE.

Mignon and for Paul Delaroche's La Gloire, met the superb Madame Sabatier, the only woman that Baudelaire loved, and the original of that extraordinary group of Clésinger's — the sculptor and son-in-law of George Sand — la Femme au Serpent, a Salammbô à la mode in marble. Hasheesh was eaten, so Gautier writes, by Boissard and Baudelaire. As for the creator of Mademoiselle Maupin, he was too robust for such nonsense. He had to work for his living at journalism, and he died in harness, an irreproachable father, while the unhappy Baudelaire, the inheritor of an intense, unstable temperament, soon devoured his patrimony of 75,000 francs, and for the remaining years of his life was between the devil of his dusky Jenny Duval and the deep sea of hopeless debt.

It was at these Pimodan gatherings, which were no doubt much less wicked than the participants would have us believe, that Baudelaire encountered Emile Deroy, a painter of skill, who made his portrait, and encouraged the fashionable young fellow to continue his art studies. We have seen an album containing sketches by the poet. They betray talent of about the same order as Thackeray's, with a superadded note of the "horrific"—that favourite epithet of the early Poe critics. Baudelaire admired Thackeray, and when the Englishman praised the illustrations of Guys, he was delighted. Deroy taught his pupil the commonplaces of a painter's technique; also how to compose a palette—a rather meaningless phrase nowadays. At least, he did not write of the arts without some technical experience. Delacroix took up his enthusiastic disciple, and when the Salons of Baudelaire appeared in 1845, 1846, 1855, and 1859, the praise and blame they evoked were testimonies to the training and knowledge of their author. A new spirit had been born.

The names of Diderot and Baudelaire were coupled. Neither academic nor spouting the jargon of the usual critic, the Salons of Baudelaire are the production of a humanist. Some would put them above Diderot's. Mr. Saintsbury, after Swinburne the warmest advocate of Baudelaire among the English, thinks that the French poet in his picture criticism observed too little and imagined too much. "In other words," he adds, " to read a criticism of Baudelaire's without the title affixed is by no means a sure method of recognizing the picture afterward." Now, word-painting was the very thing that Baudelaire avoided. It was his friend Gautier, with the plastic style, who attempted the well-nigh impossible feat of competing in his verbal descriptions with the certitudes of canvas and marble. And, if he with his verbal imagination did not entirely succeed, how could a less adept manipulator of the vocabulary? We do not agree with Mr. Saintsbury. No one can imagine too much when the imagination is that of a poet. Baudelaire divined the work of the artist and set it down scrupulously in a prose of exceeding rectitude. He did not paint pictures in prose. He did not divagate. He did not overburden his pages with technical terms. But the spirit of his subject he did disengage in a few swift phrases. The polemics of historical schools were a cross for him to bear, and he wore his prejudices lightly. Like a true critic, he judged more by form than theme. There are no types; there is only life, he asserted, and long before Jules Laforgue. He was ever art-for-art, yet, having breadth of comprehension and a Heine-like capacity for seeing both sides of his own nature with its idiosyncrasies, he could write: "The puerile utopia of the school of art-for-art, in excluding morality, and often even passion, was necessarily sterile. All literature which refuses to advance fraternally between science and philosophy is a homicidal and a suicidal literature."

Baudelaire, then, was no less sound a critic of the plastic arts than of music and literature. Like his friend Flaubert, he had a horror of democracy, of the democratisation of the arts, of all the sentimental fuss and fuddle of a pseudo-humanitarianism. During the 1848 agitation the former dandy of 1840 put on a blouse and spoke of barricades. Those things were in the air. Wagner rang the alarm-bells during the Dresden uprising. Chopin wrote for the pianoforte a revolutionary étude. Brave lads! Poets and musicians fight their battles best in the region of the ideal. Baudelaire's little attack of the equality-measles soon vanished. He lectured his brother poets and artists on the folly and injustice of abusing or despising the bourgeois (being a man of paradox, he dedicated a volume of his Salons to the bourgeois), but he would not have contradicted Mr.

CHARLES BAUDELAIRE.

George Moore for declaring that "in art the democrat is always reactionary. In 1830 the democrats were against Victor Hugo and Delacrois." And Les Fleurs du Mal, that book of opals, blood, and evil swamp-flowers, will never be savoured by the mob.

In his Souvenirs de Jeunesse, Champfleury speaks of the promenades in the Louvre he enjoyed the company with Baudelaire. Bronzino was one of the poet's preferences. He was also attracted by El Greco — not an unnatural admiration, considering the sombre extravagance of his own genius. Of Goya he has written in exalted phrases. Velasquez was his touchstone. Being of a perverse nature, his nerves ruined by abuse of drink and drugs, the landscapes of his imagination were more beautiful than Nature herself. The country itself, he declared, was odious. Like Whistler, whom he often met — see the Hommage à Delacrois by Fantin-Latour, with its portraits of Whistler, Baudelaire, Manet, Bracquemond the etcher, Legros, Delacrois, Cordier, Duranty the critic, and De Balleroy — he could not help showing his aversion to "foolish sunsets." In a word, Baudelaire, into whose brain had entered too

CHARLES BAUDELAIRE.

much moonlight, was the father of a lunar school of poetry, criticism and fiction. His Samuel Cramer, in La Fanfarlo, is the literary progenitor of Jean, Duc d'Esseintes, in Huysmans's *A Rebours*. Huysmans at first modelled himself upon Baudelaire. His Le Drageoir aux Epices is a continuation of Petits Poèmes en Prose. And to Baudelaire's account must be laid much artificial morbid writing. Despite his pursuit of perfection in form, his influence has been too often baneful to impressionable artists in embryo. A lover of Gallic Byronism, and high-priest of the Satanic school, there was no extravagance, absurd or terrible, that he did not commit, from etching a four-part fugue on ice to skating hymns in honour of Lucifer. In his criticism alone was he the sane logical Frenchman. And while he did not live to see the success of the Impressionist group, he surely would have acclaimed their theory and practice. Was he not an impressionist himself?

As Richard Wagner was his god in music, so Delacroix quite overflowed his æsthetic consciousness. Read Volume II of his collected works, *Curiosities Esthétiques*, which contains his Salons; also his essay, *De l'Essence du Rire*

CHARLES BAUDELAIRE.

(worthy to be placed side by side with George Meredith's essay on Comedy). Caricaturists, French and foreign, are considered in two chapters at the close of the volume. Baudelaire was as conscientious as Gautier. He trotted around miles of mediocre canvas, saying an encouraging word to the less talented, boiling over with holy indignation or indulging in glacial irony, before the rash usurpers occupying the seats of the mighty, and pouncing on new genius with promptitude. Upon Delacroix he lavished the largesse of his admiration. He smiled at the platitudes of Horace Vernet, and only shook his head over the Schnetzes and other artisans of the day. He welcomed William Hausollier, now so little known. He praised Devéria, Chasseriau —who waited years before he came into his own; his preferred landscapists were Corot, Rousseau and Troyon. He impolitely spoke of Ary Scheffer and the " apes of sentiment "; while his discussions of Hogarth, Cruikshank, Pinelli and Breughel proclaims his versatility of vision. In his essay Le Peintre de la Vie Moderne he was the first among critics to recognize the peculiar quality called " modernity," that naked vibration which informs the novels of Goncourt, Flaubert's L'Education Sentimentale, and the pictures of Manet, Monet, Degas and Raffaelli with their evocations of a new, nervous Paris. It is in his Volume III, entitled L'Art Romantique, that so many things dear to the new century were then subjects of furious quarrels. This book contains much just and brilliant writing. It was easy for Nietzsche to praise Wagner in Germany in 1876, but dangerous at Paris in 1861 to declare war on Wagner's adverse critics. This Baudelaire did.

The relations of Baudelaire and Edouard Manet were exceedingly cordial. In a letter to Théophile Thoré, the art critic (Letters, p. 361), we find Baudelaire defending his friend from the accusation that his pictures were pastiches of Goya. He wrote: "Manet has never seen Goya, never El Greco; he was never in the Pourtalés Gallery." Which may have been true at the time, 1864, nevertheless Manet had visited Madrid and spent much time studying Velasquez and abusing Spanish cookery. (Consider, too, Goya's Balcony with Girls and Manet's famous Balcony.) Raging at the charge of imitation, Baudelaire said in this same epistle: "They accuse even me of imitating Edgar Poe. . . . Do you know why I so patiently translated Poe? Because he resembled me." The poet italicized these words. With stupefaction, therefore, he admired the mysterious coincidences of Manet's work with that of Goya and El Greco.

He took Manet seriously. He wrote to him in a paternal and severe tone. Recall his reproof when urging the painter to exhibit his work. "You complain about attacks, but are you the first to endure them? Have you more genius than Chateaubriand and Wagner? They were not killed by derision. And in order not to make you too proud I must tell you that they are models, each in his way, and in a very rich world, while you are only the first in the decrepitude of your art." (Letters, p. 436.)

Would Baudelaire recall these prophetic words if he were able to revisit the glimpses of the Champs Elysées at the Autumn Salons? What would he think of Césanne? Odilon Redon he would understand, for he is the transposer of Baudelairianism to terms of design and colour. And perhaps the poet whose verse is saturated with tropical hues — he, when young, sailed in southern seas — might appreciate the monstrous debauch of form and colour in the Tahitian canvases of Paul Gauguin.

Baudelaire's preoccupation with pictorial themes máy be noted in his verse. He is par excellence the poet of æsthetics. To Daumier he inscribed a poem; and to the sculptor Ernest Christophe, to Delacroix (Sur Tasse en Prison), to Manet, to Guys (Rêve Parisien), to an unknown master (Une Martyre); and Watteau, a Watteau à rebours, is seen in Un Voyage à Cythère; while in Les Phares this poet of the ideal, spleen music, and perfume, shows his adoration for Rubens, Leonardo da Vinci, Michelangelo, Rembrandt, Puget, Goya, Delacroix — "Delacroix, lac de sang hanté des mauvais anges." And what is more exquisite than his quatrain to Lola de Valence, a poetic inscription for the picture of Edouard Manet, with its last line as vaporous, as subtle as Verlaine: "Le charme inattendu d'un bijou rose et noir!" Heine called himself the last of the Romantics. The first of the "Moderns" and the last of the Romantics was the many-sided Charles Baudelaire.

III

HE was born at Paris, April 9, 1821 (Flaubert's birth year), and not April 21, as Gautier has it. His father was Joseph Francis Baudelaire, or Beaudelaire, who occupied a government position. A cultivated art lover, his taste was apparent in the home he made for his second wife, Caroline Archimbaut-Dufays, an orphan and the daughter of a military officer. There was a considerable difference in the years of this pair; the mother was twenty-seven, the father sixty-two, at the birth of their only child. By his first marriage the elder Baudelaire had one son, Claude, who, like his half-brother Charles, died of paralysis, though a steady man of business. That great modern neurosis, called Commerce, has its mental wrecks, too, and no one pays attention; but when a poet falls by the wayside is the chase begun by neurologists and other soul-hunters seeking victims. After the death of Baudelaire's father, the widow, within a year, married the handsome, ambitious Aupick, then chef de bataillon, lieutenant-colonel, decorated with the Legion of Honour, and later general and ambassador to Madrid,

Constantinople, and London. Charles was a nervous, frail youth, but unlike most children of genius, he was a scholar and won brilliant honours at school. His stepfather was proud of him. From the Royal College of Lyons, Charles went to the Lycée Louis-le-Grand, Paris, but was expelled in 1839, on various discreditable charges. Troubles soon began at home. He was irascible, vain, precocious, and given to dissipation. He quarreled with General Aupick, and disdained his mother. But she was to blame, she has confessed; she had quite forgotten the boy in the flush of her second love. He could not forget, or forgive what he called her infidelity to the memory of his father. Hamlet-like, he was inconsolable. The good Bishop of Montpellier, who knew the family, said that Charles was a little crazy — second marriages usually bring woe in their train. "When a mother has such a son, she does n't re-marry," said the young poet. Charles signed himself Baudelaire-Dufays, or sometimes Dufais. He wrote in his journal: "My ancestors, idiots or maniacs . . . all victims of terrible passions"; which was one of his exaggerations. His grandfather on the paternal side was a Champenois peasant, his mother's family presumably Norman, but not much is known of her forbears. Charles believed himself lost from the time his half-brother was stricken. He also believed that his instability of temperament — and he studied his "case" as would a surgeon — was the result of his parents' disparity in years.

After his return from the East, where he did not learn English as has been said — his mother taught him as a boy to converse in and write the language — he came into his little inheritance, about fifteen thousand dollars. Two years later he was so heavily in debt that his family asked for a guardian on the ground of incompetency. He had been swindled, being young and green. How had he squandered his money? Not exactly on opera-glasses, like Gérard de Nerval, but on clothes, pictures, furniture, books. The remnant was set aside to pay his debts. Charles would be both poet and dandy. He dressed expensively but soberly, in the English fashion; his linen dazzling, the prevailing hue of his habiliments black. In height he was medium, his eyes brown, searching, luminous, the eye of a nyctalops, "eyes like ravens"; nostrils palpitating, cleft chin, mouth expressive, sensual jaw, strong and square. His hair was black, curly, glossy, his forehead high, square and white. In the Deroy portrait he wears a beard; he is there what Catulle Mendès nicknamed him: "His Excellence, Monseigneur Brummel!" Later he was the elegiac Satan, the author of L'Imitation de N. S. le Diable; or the Baudelaire of George Moore: "the clean-shaven face of the mock priest, the slow cold eyes and the sharp cunning sneer of the cynical libertine who will be tempted that he may better know the worthlessness of temptation." In the heyday of his blood he was perverse and deliberate. Let us credit him with contradicting the Byronic notion that ennui could best be cured by dissipation; in sin Baudelaire found the saddest of all consolations. Mendès laughs at the legend of Baudelaire's violence, of his being given to explosive phrases. Despite Gautier's stories about the Hôtel Pimadon and its club of hash-eaters, M. Mendès denies that Baudelaire was a victim of the hemp. What the majority of mankind does not know concerning the habits of literary workers is this prime fact: men who work hard, writing verse — and there is no mental toil comparable to it — cannot drink, or indulge in opium, without inevitable collapse. The old-fashioned ideas of " inspiration," spontaneity, easy improvisation, the sudden bolt from heaven, are delusions still hugged by the world. To be told that Chopin filed at his music for years, that Beethoven in his smithy forged his thunderbolts by the sweat of his brow, that Manet toiled like a labourer on the dock, that Baudelaire was a mechanic in his devotion to poetic work, that Gautier was a hard-working journalist, are disillusions for the sentimental. Minerva springing full-fledged from Jupiter's skull to the desk of the poet is a pretty fancy; but Balsac and Flaubert did not encourage this fancy. Work literally killed Poe, as it killed Jules de Goncourt, Flaubert and Daudet. Maupassant went insane because he would work and he would play the same day. Baudelaire worked and worried. His debts haunted him his life long. His constitution was flawed — Sainte-Beuve told him that he had worn out his nerves — from the start, he was détraqué; but that his entire life was one huge debauch is a nightmare of the moral police in some red cotton nightcap country.

CHARLES BAUDELAIRE.

His period of mental production was not brief nor barren. He was a student. Du Camp's charge that he was an ignorant man is disproved by the variety and quality of his published work. His range of sympathies was large. His mistake, in the eyes of his colleagues, was to write so well about the seven arts. Versatility is seldom given its real name — which is protracted labour. Baudelaire was one of the elect, an aristocrat, who dealt with the quintessence of art; his delicate air of a bishop, his exquisite manners, his modulated voice, aroused unusual interest and admiration. He was a humanist of distinction; he has left a hymn to Saint Francis in the Latin of the decadence. Baudelaire, like Chopin, made more poignant the phrase, raised to a higher intensity the expressiveness of art.

Women played a commanding rôle in his life. They always do with any poet worthy of the name, though few have been so frank in acknowledging this as Baudelaire. Yet he was in love more with Woman than the individual. The legend of the beautiful creature he brought from the East resolves itself into the dismal affair with Jeanne Duval. He met her in Paris, after he had been in the East. She sang at a café concert in Paris. She was more brown than black. She was not handsome, not intelligent, not good; yet he idealized her, for she was the source of half his inspiration. To her were addressed those marvellous evocations of the Orient, of perfume, tresses, delicious dawns on strange far-away seas and "superb Byzant," domes that devils built. Baudelaire is the poet of perfumes; he is also the patron saint of ennui. No one has so chanted the praise of odours. His soul swims on perfume as do other souls on music, he has sung. As he grew older he seemed to hunt for more acrid odours; he often presents an elaborately chased vase the carving of which transports us, but from which the head is quickly averted. Jeanne, whom he never loved, no matter what may be said, was a sorceress. But she was impossible; she robbed, betrayed him; he left her a dozen times only to return. He was a capital draughtsman with a strong nervous line and made many pen-and-ink drawings of her. They are not prepossessing. In her rapid decline she was not allowed to want. Madame Aupick paid her expenses in the hospital. A sordid history. She was a veritable flower of evil for Baudelaire. Yet poetry, like music, would be colourless, scentless, if it sounded no dissonances. Fancy art reduced to the beatific and banal chord of C major!

He fell in love with the celebrated Madame Sabatier, a reigning beauty, at whose salon artistic Paris assembled. She had been christened by Gautier Madame la Presidente, and her sumptuous beauty was portrayed by Ricard in his La Femme au Chien. She returned Baudelaire's love. They soon parted. Again a riddle which the published letters hardly solve. One letter, however, does show that Baudelaire had tried to be faithful, and failed. He could not extort from his exhausted soul the sentiment; but he put its music on paper. His most seductive lyrics were addressed to Madame Sabatier: "A la très chère, à la très-belle," a hymn saturated with love. Music, spleen, perfumes — "colour, sound, perfumes call to each other as deep to deep; perfumes like the flesh of children, soft as hautboys, green as the meadows" — criminals, outcasts, the charm of childhood, the horrors of love, pride, and rebellion, Eastern landscapes, cats, soothing and false; cats, the true companions of lonely poets; haunted

CHARLES BAUDELAIRE.

clocks, shivering dusks, and gloomier dawns — Paris in a hundred phases — these and many other themes this strange-souled poet, this "Dante, pacer of the shore," of Paris has celebrated in finely wrought verse and profound phrases. In a single line he contrives atmosphere; the very shape of his sentence, the ring of the syllables, arouse the deepest emotion. A master of harmonic undertones is Baudelaire. His successors have excelled him in making their music more fluid, more lyrical, more vapourous — many young French poets pass through their Baudelarian green-sickness — but he alone knows the secrets of moulding those metallic, free sonnets, which have the resistance of bronze; and of the despairing music that flames from the mouths of lost souls trembling on the wharves of hell. He is the supreme master of irony and troubled voluptuousness.

Baudelaire is a masculine poet. He carved rather than sang; the plastic arts spoke to his soul. A lover and maker of images. Like Poe, his emotions transformed themselves into ideas. Bourget classified him as mystic, libertine, and analyst. He was born with a wound in his soul, to use the phrase of Père Lacordaire. (Curiously enough, he actually contemplated, in 1861, becoming a candidate for Lacordaire's vacant seat in the French Academy. Sainte-Beuve dissuaded him from this folly.) Recall Baudelaire's prayer: " Thou, O Lord, my God, grant me the grace to produce some fine lines which will prove to myself that I am not the last of men, that 1 am not inferior to those I contemn." Individualist, egoist, anarchist, his only thought was letters. Jules Laforgue thus described Baudelaire: " Cat, Hindoo, Yankee, Episcopal, Alchemist." Yes, an alchemist who suffocated in the fumes he created. He was of Gothic imagination, and could have said with Rolla: " Ja suis venu trop tard dans un monde trop vieux." He had an unassuaged thirst for the absolute. The human soul was his stage, he its interpreting orchestra.

In 1857 The Flowers of Evil was published by Poulet-Malassis, who afterward went into bankruptcy — a warning to publishers with a taste for fine literature. The titles contemplated were Limbes, or Lesbiennes. Hippolyte Babou suggested the one we know. These poems were suppressed on account of six, and poet and publisher summoned. As the mu-

nicipal government had made a particular ass
of itself in the prosecution of Gustave Flaubert
and his Madame Bovary, the Baudelaire matter
was disposed of in haste. He was condemned
to a fine of three hundred francs, a fine which
was never paid, as the objectionable poems were
removed. They were printed in the Belgian
edition, and may be read in the new volume,
Œuvres Posthumes.

Baudelaire was infuriated over the judgment,
for he knew that his book was dramatic in ex-
pression. He had expected, like Flaubert, to
emerge from the trial with flying colours; there-
fore to be classed as one who wrote objection-
able literature was a shock. " Flaubert had the
Empress back of him," he complained; which
was true; the Empress Eugénie, also the Prin-
cess Mathilde. But he worked as ever and put
forth those polished intaglios called Poems in
Prose, for the form of which he had taken a
hint from Aloys Bertrand's Gaspard de la Nuit.
He filled this form with a new content; not
alone pictures, but moods, are to be found in
those miniatures. Pity is their keynote, a ten-
derness for the abject and lowly, a revelation
of sensibility that surprised those critics who

had discerned in Baudelaire only a sculptor of
evil. In one of his poems he described a land-
scape of metal, of marble and water; a babel of
staircases and arcades, a palace of infinity, sur-
rounded by the silence of eternity. This de-
pressing yet magical dream was utilized by
Huysmans in his A Rebours. But in the tiny
landscapes of the Prose Poems there is nothing
rigid or artificial. Indeed, the poet's deliberate
attitude of artificiality is dropped. He is
human. Not that the deep fundamental note
of humanity is ever absent in his poems; the
eternal diapason is there even when least over-
heard. Baudelaire is more human than Poe.
His range of sympathy is wider. In this he
transcends him as a poet, though his subject-
matter often issues from the very dregs of life.
Brother to pitiable wanderers, there are, never-
theless, no traces of cant, no " Russian pity "
à la Dostoiëvsky, no humanitarian or socialistic
rhapsodies in his work. Baudelaire is an egoist.
He hated the sentimental sapping of altruism.
His prose-poem, Crowds, with its " bath of mul-
titude," may have been suggested by Poe; but
in Charles Lamb we find the idea: " Are there
no solitudes out of caves and the desert? or can-

not the heart, in the midst of crowds, feel frightfully alone? "

His best critical work is the Richard Wagner and Tannhauser, as significant an essay as Nietzsche's Richard Wagner in Bayreuth. And Baudelaire's polemic appeared at a more critical period in Wagner's career. Wagner sent a brief hearty letter of thanks to the critic, and later made his acquaintance. To Wagner, Baudelaire introduced a young Wagnerian, Villiers de l'Isle Adam. This Wagner letter is included in the volume of Crépet; but there are no letters published from Baudelaire to Franz Liszt, though they were friends. In Weimar I saw at the Liszt Museum several from Baudelaire which should have been included in the Letters. The poet understood Liszt and his reforms as he understood Wagner. The German composer admired the French poet, and his Kundry, in the sultry second act of Parsifal, has a Baudelairian hue, especially in the temptation scene.

The end was at hand. Baudelaire had been steadily, rather, unsteadily, going downhill; a desperate figure, a dandy in shabby attire. He went out only after dark, he haunted the exterior boulevards, associated with birds of nocturnal plumage. He drank without thirst, ate without hunger, as he has said. A woeful decadence for this aristocrat of life and letters. Most sorrowful of sinners, a morose delectation scourged his nerves and extorted the darkest music from his lyre. He fled to Brussels, there to rehabilitate his dwindling fortunes. He gave a few lectures, and met Rops, Lemonnier, drank to forget, and forgot to work. He abused Brussels, Belgium, its people. A country, he cried, where the trees are black, the flowers without odour, and where there is no conversation! He, the brilliant causeur, the chief blaguer of a circle in which young James McNeill Whistler was reduced to the rôle of a listener — this most spiritual among artists, found himself a failure in the Belgian capital. It may not be amiss to remind ourselves that Baudelaire was the creator of many of the paradoxes attributed, not only to Whistler, but to an entire school — if one may employ such a phrase. The frozen imperturbability of the poet, his cutting enunciation, his power of blasphemy, his hatred of Nature, his love of the artificial, have been copied by the æsthetic blades of our day. He it was who first taunted Nature with being an imitator of art, with always being the same. Oh, the imitative sunsets! Oh, the quotidian eating and drinking! And as pessimist, too, he led the mode. Baudelaire, like Flaubert, grasped the murky torch of pessimism once held by Chateaubriand, Benjamin Constant, and Senancour. Doubtless, all this stemmed from Byronism. And now it is as stale as Byronism.

His health failed, and he lacked money enough to pay for doctor's prescriptions; he even owed for the room in his hotel. At Namur, where he was visiting the father-in-law of Felician Rops (March, 1866), he suffered from an attack of paralysis. He was removed to Brussels. His mother, who lived at Honfleur, in mourning for her husband, came to his aid. Taken to France, he was placed in a sanatorium. Aphasia set in. He could only ejaculate a mild oath, and when he caught sight of himself in the mirror he would bow pleasantly as if to a stranger. His friends rallied, and they were among the most distinguished people in Paris, the élite of souls. Ladies visited him, one or two playing Wagner on the piano—

which must have added a fresh nuance to death — and they brought him flowers. He expressed his love for flowers and music to the last. He could not bear the sight of his mother; she revived in him some painful memories, but that passed, and he clamoured for her when she was absent. If anyone mentioned the names of Wagner or Manet, he smiled. And with a fixed stare, as if peering through some invisible window opening upon eternity, he died, August 31, 1867, aged forty-six.

Barbey d'Aurevilly himself a Satanist and dandy (oh, those comical old attitudes of literature), had prophesied that the author of Fleurs du Mal would either blow out his brains or prostrate himself at the foot of the cross. (Later he said the same of Huysmans.) Baudelaire had the alternative course forced upon him by fate after he had attempted spiritual suicide for how many years? (He once tried actual suicide, but the slight cut in his throat looked so ugly to him that he went no farther.) His soul had been a battle-field for the powers of good and evil. That at the end he brought the wreck of both soul and body to his God should not be a subject for comment. He was an ex-

CHARLES BAUDELAIRE.

traordinary poet with a bad conscience, who lived miserably and was buried with honours. Then it was that his worth was discovered (funeral orations over a genius are a species of public staircase-wit). His reputation waxes with the years. He is an exotic gem in the crown of French poetry. Of him Swinburne has chanted Ave Atque Vale:

> Shall I strew on thee rose or rue or laurel,
> Brother, on this that was the veil of thee?

THE FLOWERS OF EVIL

THE DANCE OF DEATH.

CARRYING bouquet, and handkerchief, and gloves,
Proud of her height as when she lived, she moves
With all the careless and high-stepping grace,
And the extravagant courtesan's thin face.

Was slimmer waist e'er in a ball-room wooed?
Her floating robe, in royal amplitude,
Falls in deep folds around a dry foot, shod
With a bright flower-like shoe that gems the sod.

The swarms that hum about her collar-bones
As the lascivious streams caress the stones,
Conceal from every scornful jest that flies,
Her gloomy beauty; and her fathomless eyes

Are made of shade and void; with flowery sprays
Her skull is wreathed artistically, and sways,
Feeble and weak, on her frail vertebræ.
O charm of nothing decked in folly! they

Who laugh and name you a Caricature,
They see not, they whom flesh and blood allure,
The nameless grace of every bleached. bare bone
That is most dear to me, tall skeleton!

THE DANCE OF DEATH.

Come you to trouble with your potent sneer
The feast of Life! or are you driven here,
To Pleasure's Sabbath, by dead lusts that stir
And goad your moving corpse on with a spur?

Or do you hope, when sing the violins,
And the pale candle-flame lights up our sins,
To drive some mocking nightmare far apart,
And cool the flame hell lighted in your heart?

Fathomless well of fault and foolishness!
Eternal alembic of antique distress!
Still o'er the curved, white trellis of your sides
The sateless, wandering serpent curls and glides.

And truth to tell, I fear lest you should find,
Among us here, no lover to your mind;
Which of these hearts beat for the smile you gave?
The charms of horror please none but the brave.

Your eyes' black gulf, where awful broodings stir,
Brings giddiness; the prudent reveller
Sees, while a horror grips him from beneath,
The eternal smile of thirty-two white teeth.

For he who has not folded in his arms
A skeleton, nor fed on graveyard charms,
Recks not of furbelow, or paint, or scent,
When Horror comes the way that Beauty went.

[4]

THE DANCE OF DEATH.

O irresistible, with fleshless face,
Say to these dancers in their dazzled race:
"Proud lovers with the paint above your bones,
Ye shall taste death, musk-scented skeletons!

Withered Antinoüs, dandies with plump faces,
Ye varnished cadavers, and grey Lovelaces,
Ye go to lands unknown and void of breath,
Drawn by the rumour of the Dance of Death.

From Seine's cold quays to Ganges' burning stream,
The mortal troupes dance onward in a dream;
They do not see, within the opened sky,
The Angel's sinister trumpet raised on high.

In every clime and under every sun,
Death laughs at ye, mad mortals, as ye run;
And oft perfumes herself with myrrh, like ye
And mingles with your madness, irony!"

THE BEACONS.

RUBENS, oblivious garden of indolence,
    Pillow of cool flesh where no man dreams of love,
Where life flows forth in troubled opulence,
    As airs in heaven and seas in ocean move.

LEONARD DA VINCI, sombre and fathomless glass,
    Where lovely angels with calm lips that smile,
Heavy with mystery, in the shadow pass,
    Among the ice and pines that guard some isle.

REMBRANDT, sad hospital that a murmuring fills,
    Where one tall crucifix hangs on the walls,
Where every tear-drowned prayer some woe distils,
    And one cold, wintry ray obliquely falls.

Strong MICHELANGELO, a vague far place
    Where mingle Christs with pagan Hercules;
Thin phantoms of the great through twilight pace,
    And tear their shroud with clenched hands void
        of ease.

The fighter's anger, the faun's impudence,
    Thou makest of all these a lovely thing;
Proud heart, sick body, mind's magnificence:
    PUGET, the convict's melancholy king.

THE BEACONS.

WATTEAU, the carnival of illustrious hearts,
  Fluttering like moths upon the wings of chance;
Bright lustres light the silk that flames and darts,
  And pour down folly on the whirling dance.

GOYA, a nightmare full of things unknown;
  The fœtus witches broil on Sabbath night;
Old women at the mirror; children lone
  Who tempt old demons with their limbs delight.

DELACROIX, lake of blood ill angels haunt,
  Where ever-green, o'ershadowing woods arise;
Under the surly heaven strange fanfares chaunt
  And pass, like one of Weber's strangled sighs.

And malediction, blasphemy and groan,
  Ecstasies, cries, Te Deums, and tears of brine,
Are echoes through a thousand labyrinths flown;
  For mortal hearts an opiate divine;

A shout cried by a thousand sentinels,
  An order from a thousand bugles tossed,
A beacon o'er a thousand citadels,
  A call to huntsmen in deep woodlands lost.

It is the mightiest witness that could rise
  To prove our dignity, O Lord, to Thee;
This sob that rolls from age to age, and dies
  Upon the verge of Thy Eternity!

THE SADNESS OF THE MOON.

THE Moon more indolently dreams to-night
Than a fair woman on her couch at rest,
Caressing, with a hand distraught and light,
Before she sleeps, the contour of her breast.

Upon her silken avalanche of down,
Dying she breathes a long and swooning sigh;
And watches the white visions past her flown,
Which rise like blossoms to the azure sky.

And when, at times, wrapped in her languor deep,
Earthward she lets a furtive tear-drop flow,
Some pious poet, enemy of sleep,

Takes in his hollow hand the tear of snow
Whence gleams of iris and of opal start,
And hides it from the Sun, deep in his heart.

EXOTIC PERFUME.

WHEN with closed eyes in autumn's eves of gold
  I breathe the burning odours of your breast,
  Before my eyes the hills of happy rest
Bathed in the sun's monotonous fires, unfold.

Islands of Lethe where exotic boughs
  Bend with their burden of strange fruit bowed down,
  Where men are upright, maids have never grown
Unkind, but bear a light upon their brows.

Led by that perfume to these lands of ease,
I see a port where many ships have flown
With sails outwearied of the wandering seas;

While the faint odours from green tamarisks blown,
Float to my soul and in my senses throng,
And mingle vaguely with the sailor's song.

BEAUTY.

I AM as lovely as a dream in stone,
And this my heart where each finds death in turn,
Inspires the poet with a love as lone
As clay eternal and as taciturn.

Swan-white of heart, a sphinx no mortal knows,
My throne is in the heaven's azure deep;
I hate all movements that disturb my pose,
I smile not ever, neither do I weep.

Before my monumental attitudes,
That breathe a soul into the plastic arts,
My poets pray in austere studious moods,

For I, to fold enchantment round their hearts.
Have pools of light where beauty flames and dies,
The placid mirrors of my luminous eyes.

THE BALCONY.

MOTHER of memories, mistress of mistresses,
  O thou, my pleasure, thou, all my desire,
Thou shalt recall the beauty of caresses,
  The charm of evenings by the gentle fire,
Mother of memories, mistress of mistresses!

The eves illumined by the burning coal,
  The balcony where veiled rose-vapour clings —
How soft your breast was then, how sweet your soul!
  Ah, and we said imperishable things,
Those eves illumined by the burning coal.

Lovely the suns were in those twilights warm,
  And space profound, and strong life's pulsing flood,
In bending o'er you, queen of every charm,
  I thought I breathed the perfume in your blood.
The suns were beauteous in those twilights warm.

The film of night flowed round and over us,
  And my eyes in the dark did your eyes meet;
I drank your breath, ah! sweet and poisonous,
  And in my hands fraternal slept your feet —
Night, like a film, flowed round and over us.

[11]

THE BALCONY.

I can recall those happy days forgot,
   And see, with head bowed on your knees, my past.
Your languid beauties now would move me not
   Did not your gentle heart and body cast
The old spell of those happy days forgot.

Can vows and perfumes, kisses infinite,
   Be reborn from the gulf we cannot sound;
As rise to heaven suns once again made bright
   After being plunged in deep seas and profound?
Ah, vows and perfumes, kisses infinite!

THE SICK MUSE.

Poor Muse, alas, what ails thee, then, to-day?
Thy hollow eyes with midnight visions burn,
Upon thy brow in alternation play,
Folly and Horror, cold and taciturn.

Have the green lemure and the goblin red,
Poured on thee love and terror from their urn?
Or with despotic hand the nightmare dread
Deep plunged thee in some fabulous Minturne?

Would that thy breast where so deep thoughts arise,
Breathed forth a healthful perfume with thy sighs;
Would that thy Christian blood ran wave by wave

In rhythmic sounds the antique numbers gave,
When Phœbus shared his alternating reign
With mighty Pan, lord of the ripening grain.

THE VENAL MUSE.

Muse of my heart, lover of palaces,
  When January comes with wind and sleet,
During the snowy eve's long wearinesses,
  Will there be fire to warm thy violet feet!

Wilt thou reanimate thy marble shoulders
  In the moon-beams that through the window fly?
Or when thy purse dries up, thy palace moulders,
  Reap the far star-gold of the vaulted sky?

For thou, to keep thy body to thy soul,
Must swing a censer, wear a holy stole,
  And chaunt Te Deums with unbelief between.

Or, like a starving mountebank, expose
Thy beauty and thy tear-drowned smile to those
  Who wait thy jests to drive away thy spleen.

THE EVIL MONK.

THE ancient cloisters on their lofty walls
  Had holy Truth in painted frescoes shown,
And, seeing these, the pious in those halls
  Felt their cold, lone austereness less alone.

At that time when Christ's seed flowered all around,
  More than one monk, forgotten in his hour,
Taking for studio the burial-ground,
  Glorified Death with simple faith and power.

And my soul is a sepulchre where I,
Ill cenobite, have spent eternity:
  On the vile cloister walls no pictures rise.

O when may I cast off this weariness,
And make the pageant of my old distress
  For these hands labour, pleasure for these eyes?

THE TEMPTATION.

The Demon, in my chamber high,
    This morning came to visit me,
And, thinking he would find some fault,
    He whispered: "I would know of thee

Among the many lovely things
    That make the magic of her face,
Among the beauties, black and rose,
    That make her body's charm and grace,

Which is most fair?" Thou didst reply
    To the Abhorred, O soul of mine:
"No single beauty is the best
    When she is all one flower divine.

When all things charm me I ignore
    Which one alone brings most delight;
She shines before me like the dawn,
    And she consoles me like the night.

The harmony is far too great,
    That governs all her body fair,
For impotence to analyse
    And say which note is sweetest there.

THE TEMPTATION.

O mystic metamorphosis!
   My senses into one sense flow —
Her voice makes perfume when she speaks,
   Her breath is music faint and low!"

THE IRREPARABLE.

Can we suppress the old Remorse
  Who bends our heart beneath his stroke,
Who feeds, as worms feed on the corse,
  Or as the acorn on the oak?
Can we suppress the old Remorse?

Ah, in what philtre, wine, or spell,
  May we drown this our ancient foe,
Destructive glutton, gorging well,
  Patient as the ants, and slow?
What wine, what philtre, or what spell?

Tell it, enchantress, if you can,
  Tell me, with anguish overcast,
Wounded, as a dying man,
  Beneath the swift hoofs hurrying past.
Tell it, enchantress, if you can,

To him the wolf already tears
  Who sees the carrion pinions wave,
This broken warrior who despairs
  To have a cross above his grave —
This wretch the wolf already tears.

THE IRREPARABLE.

Can one illume a leaden sky,
  Or tear apart the shadowy veil
Thicker than pitch, no star on high,
  Not one funereal glimmer pale
Can one illume a leaden sky?

Hope lit the windows of the Inn,
  But now that shining flame is dead;
And how shall martyred pilgrims win
  Along the moonless road they tread?
Satan has darkened all the Inn!

Witch, do you love accursèd hearts?
  Say, do you know the reprobate?
Know you Remorse, whose venomed darts
  Make souls the targets for their hate?
Witch, do you know accursèd hearts?

The Might-have-been with tooth accursed
  Gnaws at the piteous souls of men,
The deep foundations suffer first,
  And all the structure crumbles then
Beneath the bitter tooth accursed.

THE IRREPARABLE.

II.

Often, when seated at the play,
  And sonorous music lights the stage,
I see the frail hand of a Fay
  With magic dawn illume the rage
Of the dark sky. Oft at the play

A being made of gauze and fire
  Casts to the earth a Demon great.
And my heart, whence all hopes expire,
  Is like a stage where I await,
In vain, the Fay with wings of fire!

A FORMER LIFE.

Long since, I lived beneath vast porticoes,
By many ocean-sunsets tinged and fired,
Where mighty pillars, in majestic rows,
Seemed like basaltic caves when day expired.

The rolling surge that mirrored all the skies
Mingled its music, turbulent and rich,
Solemn and mystic, with the colours which
The setting sun reflected in my eyes.

And there I lived amid voluptuous calms,
In splendours of blue sky and wandering wave,
Tended by many a naked, perfumed slave,

Who fanned my languid brow with waving palms.
They were my slaves — the only care they had
To know what secret grief had made me sad.

DON JUAN IN HADES.

WHEN Juan sought the subterranean flood,
  And paid his obolus on the Stygian shore,
Charon, the proud and sombre beggar, stood
  With one strong, vengeful hand on either oar.

With open robes and bodies agonised,
  Lost women writhed beneath that darkling sky;
There were sounds as of victims sacrificed:
  Behind him all the dark was one long cry.

And Sganarelle, with laughter, claimed his pledge;
  Don Luis, with trembling finger in the air,
Showed to the souls who wandered in the sedge
  The evil son who scorned his hoary hair.

Shivering with woe, chaste Elvira the while,
  Near him untrue to all but her till now,
Seemed to beseech him for one farewell smile
  Lit with the sweetness of the first soft vow.

And clad in armour, a tall man of stone
  Held firm the helm, and clove the gloomy flood;
But, staring at the vessel's track alone,
  Bent on his sword the unmoved hero stood.

THE LIVING FLAME.

THEY pass before me, these Eyes full of light,
Eyes made magnetic by some angel wise;
The holy brothers pass before my sight,
And cast their diamond fires in my dim eyes.

They keep me from all sin and error grave,
They set me in the path whence Beauty came;
They are my servants, and I am their slave,
And all my soul obeys the living flame.

Beautiful Eyes that gleam with mystic light
As candles lighted at full noon; the sun
Dims not your flame phantastical and bright.

You sing the dawn; they celebrate life done;
Marching you chaunt my soul's awakening hymn,
Stars that no sun has ever made grow dim!

CORRESPONDENCES.

In Nature's temple living pillars rise,
  And words are murmured none have understood,
  And man must wander through a tangled wood
Of symbols watching him with friendly eyes.

As long-drawn echoes heard far-off and dim
  Mingle to one deep sound and fade away;
  Vast as the night and brilliant as the day,
Colour and sound and perfume speak to him.

Some perfumes are as fragrant as a child,
  Sweet as the sound of hautboys, meadow-green;
Others, corrupted, rich, exultant, wild,

Have all the expansion of things infinite:
  As amber, incense, musk, and benzoin,
Which sing the sense's and the soul's delight.

THE FLASK.

THERE are some powerful odours that can pass
Out of the stoppered flagon; even glass
To them is porous. Oft when some old box
Brought from the East is opened and the locks
And hinges creak and cry; or in a press
In some deserted house, where the sharp stress
Of odours old and dusty fills the brain;
An ancient flask is brought to light again,
And forth the ghosts of long-dead odours creep.
There, softly trembling in the shadows, sleep
A thousand thoughts, funereal chrysalides,
Phantoms of old the folding darkness hides,
Who make faint flutterings as their wings unfold,
Rose-washed and azure-tinted, shot with gold.

A memory that brings languor flutters here:
The fainting eyelids droop, and giddy Fear
Thrusts with both hands the soul towards the pit
Where, like a Lazarus from his winding-sheet,
Arises from the gulf of sleep a ghost
Of an old passion, long since loved and lost.

THE FLASK.

So I, when vanished from man's memory
Deep in some dark and sombre chest I lie,
An empty flagon they have cast aside,
Broken and soiled, the dust upon my pride,
Will be your shroud, beloved pestilence!
The witness of your might and virulence,
Sweet poison mixed by angels; bitter cup
Of life and death my heart has drunken up!

REVERSIBILITY.

ANGEL of gaiety, have you tasted grief?
  Shame and remorse and sobs and weary spite,
  And the vague terrors of the fearful night
That crush the heart up like a crumpled leaf?
Angel of gaiety, have you tasted grief?

Angel of kindness, have you tasted hate?
  With hands clenched in the shade and tears of gall,
  When Vengeance beats her hellish battle-call,
And makes herself the captain of our fate,
Angel of kindness, have you tasted hate?

Angel of health, did ever you know pain,
  Which like an exile trails his tired footfalls
  The cold length of the white infirmary walls,
With lips compressed, seeking the sun in vain?
Angel of health, did ever you know pain?

Angel of beauty, do you wrinkles know?
  Know you the fear of age, the torment vile
  Of reading secret horror in the smile
Of eyes your eyes have loved since long ago?
Angel of beauty, do you wrinkles know?

REVERSIBILITY.

Angel of happiness, and joy, and light,
  Old David would have asked for youth afresh
  From the pure touch of your enchanted flesh;
I but implore your prayers to aid my plight,
Angel of happiness, and joy, and light.

THE EYES OF BEAUTY.

You are a sky of autumn, pale and rose;
But all the sea of sadness in my blood
Surges, and ebbing, leaves my lips morose,
Salt with the memory of the bitter flood.

In vain your hand glides my faint bosom o'er,
That which you seek, beloved, is desecrate
By woman's tooth and talon; ah, no more
Seek in me for a heart which those dogs ate.

It is a ruin where the jackals rest,
And rend and tear and glut themselves and slay —
A perfume swims about your naked breast!

Beauty, hard scourge of spirits, have your way!
With flame-like eyes that at bright feasts have flared
Burn up these tatters that the beasts have spared!

SONNET OF AUTUMN.

They say to me, thy clear and crystal eyes:
  "Why dost thou love me so, strange lover mine?"
Be sweet, be still! My heart and soul despise
  All save that antique brute-like faith of thine;

And will not bare the secret of their shame
  To thee whose hand soothes me to slumbers long,
Nor their black legend write for thee in flame!
  Passion I hate, a spirit does me wrong.

Let us love gently. Love, from his retreat,
Ambushed and shadowy, bends his fatal bow,
And I too well his ancient arrows know:

Crime, horror, folly. O pale marguerite,
Thou art as I, a bright sun fallen low,
O my so white, my so cold Marguerite.

THE REMORSE OF THE DEAD.

O SHADOWY Beauty mine, when thou shalt sleep
  In the deep heart of a black marble tomb;
When thou for mansion and for bower shalt keep
  Only one rainy cave of hollow gloom;

And when the stone upon thy trembling breast,
  And on thy straight sweet body's supple grace,
Crushes thy will and keeps thy heart at rest,
  And holds those feet from their adventurous race;

Then the deep grave, who shares my reverie,
(For the deep grave is aye the poet's friend)
During long nights when sleep is far from thee,

Shall whisper: "Ah, thou didst not comprehend
The dead wept thus, thou woman frail and weak"—
And like remorse the worm shall gnaw thy cheek.

THE GHOST.

SOFTLY as brown-eyed Angels rove
I will return to thy alcove,
And glide upon the night to thee,
Treading the shadows silently.

And I will give to thee, my own,
Kisses as icy as the moon,
And the caresses of a snake
Cold gliding in the thorny brake.

And when returns the livid morn
Thou shalt find all my place forlorn
And chilly, till the falling night.

Others would rule by tenderness
Over thy life and youthfulness,
But I would conquer thee by fright!

TO A MADONNA.

(*An Ex-Voto in the Spanish taste.*)

MADONNA, mistress, I would build for thee
An altar deep in the sad soul of me;
And in the darkest corner of my heart,
From mortal hopes and mocking eyes apart,
Carve of enamelled blue and gold a shrine
For thee to stand erect in, Image divine!
And with a mighty Crown thou shalt be crowned
Wrought of the gold of my smooth Verse, set round
With starry crystal rhymes; and I will make,
O mortal maid, a Mantle for thy sake,
And weave it of my jealousy, a gown
Heavy, barbaric, stiff, and weighted down
With my distrust, and broider round the hem
Not pearls, but all my tears in place of them.
And then thy wavering, trembling robe shall be
All the desires that rise and fall in me
From mountain-peaks to valleys of repose,
Kissing thy lovely body's white and rose.
For thy humiliated feet divine,
Of my Respect I'll make thee Slippers fine
Which, prisoning them within a gentle fold,

[33]

TO A MADONNA.

Shall keep their imprint like a faithful mould.
And if my art, unwearying and discreet,
Can make no Moon of Silver for thy feet
To have for Footstool, then thy heel shall rest
Upon the snake that gnaws within my breast,
Victorious Queen of whom our hope is born!
And thou shalt trample down and make a scorn
Of the vile reptile swollen up with hate.
And thou shalt see my thoughts, all consecrate,
Like candles set before thy flower-strewn shrine,
O Queen of Virgins, and the taper-shine
Shall glimmer star-like in the vault of blue,
With eyes of flame for ever watching you.
While all the love and worship in my sense
Will be sweet smoke of myrrh and frankincense.
Ceaselessly up to thee, white peak of snow,
My stormy spirit will in vapours go!

And last, to make thy drama all complete,
That love and cruelty may mix and meet,
I, thy remorseful torturer, will take
All the Seven Deadly Sins, and from them make
In darkest joy, Seven Knives, cruel-edged and keen,
'And like a juggler choosing, O my Queen,
That spot profound whence love and mercy start,
I'll plunge them all within thy panting heart!

THE SKY.

WHERE'ER he be, on water or on land,
  Under pale suns or climes that flames enfold;
One of Christ's own, or of Cythera's band,
  Shadowy beggar or Crœsus rich with gold;

Citizen, peasant, student, tramp; whate'er
  His little brain may be, alive or dead;
Man knows the fear of mystery everywhere,
  And peeps, with trembling glances, overhead.

The heaven above? A strangling cavern wall;
The lighted ceiling of a music-hall
  Where every actor treads a bloody soil —

The hermit's hope; the terror of the sot;
The sky: the black lid of the mighty pot
  Where the vast human generations boil!

SPLEEN.

I'M like some king in whose corrupted veins
Flows agèd blood; who rules a land of rains;
Who, young in years, is old in all distress;
Who flees good counsel to find weariness
Among his dogs and playthings, who is stirred
Neither by hunting-hound nor hunting-bird;
Whose weary face emotion moves no more
E'en when his people die before his door.
His favourite Jester's most fantastic wile
Upon that sick, cruel face can raise no smile;
The courtly dames, to whom all kings are good,
Can lighten this young skeleton's dull mood
No more with shameless toilets. In his gloom
Even his lilied bed becomes a tomb.
The sage who takes his gold essays in vain
To purge away the old corrupted strain,
His baths of blood, that in the days of old
The Romans used when their hot blood grew cold,
Will never warm this dead man's bloodless pains,
For green Lethean water fills his veins.

THE OWLS.

UNDER the overhanging yews,
The dark owls sit in solemn state,
Like stranger gods; by twos and twos
Their red eyes gleam. They meditate.

Motionless thus they sit and dream
Until that melancholy hour
When, with the sun's last fading gleam,
The nightly shades assume their power.

From their still attitude the wise
Will learn with terror to despise
All tumult, movement, and unrest;

For he who follows every shade,
Carries the memory in his breast,
Of each unhappy journey made.

BIEN LOIN D'ICI.

HERE is the chamber consecrate,
Wherein this maiden delicate,
And enigmatically sedate,

Fans herself while the moments creep,
Upon her cushions half-asleep,
And hears the fountains plash and weep.

Dorothy's chamber undefiled.
The winds and waters sing afar
Their song of sighing strange and wild
To lull to sleep the petted child.

From head to foot with subtle care,
Slaves have perfumed her delicate skin
With odorous oils and benzoin.
And flowers faint in a corner there.

MUSIC.

Music doth oft uplift me like a sea
   Towards my planet pale,
Then through dark fogs or heaven's infinity
   I lift my wandering sail.

With breast advanced, drinking the winds that flee,
   And through the cordage wail,
I mount the hurrying waves night hides from me
   Beneath her sombre veil.

I feel the tremblings of all passions known
   To ships before the breeze;
Cradled by gentle winds, or tempest-blown

   I pass the abysmal seas
That are, when calm, the mirror level and fair
   Of my despair!

CONTEMPLATION.

THOU, O my Grief, be wise and tranquil still,
The eve is thine which even now drops down,
To carry peace or care to human will,
And in a misty veil enfolds the town.

While the vile mortals of the multitude,
By pleasure, cruel tormentor, goaded on,
Gather remorseful blossoms in light mood —
Grief, place thy hand in mine, let us be gone

Far from them. Lo, see how the vanished years,
In robes outworn lean over heaven's rim:
And from the water, smiling through her tears,

Remorse arises, and the sun grows dim;
And in the east, her long shroud trailing light,
List, O my grief, the gentle steps of Night.

TO A BROWN BEGGAR-MAID.

WHITE maiden with the russet hair,
Whose garments, through their holes, declare
That poverty is part of you,
    And beauty too.

To me, a sorry bard and mean,
Your youthful beauty, frail and lean,
With summer freckles here and there,
    Is sweet and fair.

Your sabots tread the roads of chance,
And not one queen of old romance
Carried her velvet shoes and lace
    With half your grace.

In place of tatters far too short
Let the proud garments worn at Court
Fall down with rustling fold and pleat
    About your feet;

In place of stockings, worn and old,
Let a keen dagger all of gold
Gleam in your garter for the eyes
    Of roués wise;

TO A BROWN BEGGAR-MAID.

Let ribbons carelessly untied
Reveal to us the radiant pride
Of your white bosom purer far
    Than any star;

Let your white arms uncovered shine,
Polished and smooth and half divine;
And let your elfish fingers chase
    With riotous grace

The purest pearls that softly glow,
The sweetest sonnets of Belleau,
Offered by gallants ere they fight
    For your delight;

And many fawning rhymers who
Inscribe their first thin book to you
Will contemplate upon the stair
    Your slipper fair;

And many a page who plays at cards,
And many lords and many bards,
Will watch your going forth, and burn
    For your return;

And you will count before your glass
More kisses than the lily has;
And more than one Valois will sigh
    When you pass by.

TO A BROWN BEGGAR–MAID.

But meanwhile you are on the tramp,
Begging your living in the damp,
Wandering mean streets and alleys o'er,
    From door to door;

And shilling bangles in a shop
Cause you with eager eyes to stop,
And I, alas, have not a sou
    To give to you.

Then go, with no more ornament,
Pearl, diamond, or subtle scent,
Than your own fragile naked grace
    And lovely face.

THE SWAN.

ANDROMACHE, I think of you! The stream,
The poor, sad mirror where in bygone days
Shone all the majesty of your widowed grief,
The lying Simoïs flooded by your tears,
Made all my fertile memory blossom forth
As I passed by the new-built Carrousel.
Old Paris is no more (a town, alas,
Changes more quickly than man's heart may change);
Yet in my mind I still can see the booths;
The heaps of brick and rough-hewn capitals;
The grass; the stones all over-green with moss;
The *débris*, and the square-set heaps of tiles.

There a menagerie was once outspread;
And there I saw, one morning at the hour
When toil awakes beneath the cold, clear sky,
And the road roars upon the silent air,
A swan who had escaped his cage, and walked
On the dry pavement with his webby feet,
And trailed his spotless plumage on the ground.

[44]

THE SWAN.

And near a waterless stream the piteous swan
Opened his beak, and bathing in the dust
His nervous wings, he cried (his heart the while
Filled with a vision of his own fair lake):
"O water, when then wilt thou come in rain?
Lightning, when wilt thou glitter?"

                          Sometimes yet
I see the hapless bird — strange, fatal myth —
Like him that Ovid writes of, lifting up
Unto the cruelly blue, ironic heavens,
With stretched, convulsive neck a thirsty face,
As though he sent reproaches up to God!

II.

Paris may change; my melancholy is fixed.
New palaces, and scaffoldings, and blocks,
And suburbs old, are symbols all to me
Whose memories are as heavy as a stone.
And so, before the Louvre, to vex my soul,
The image came of my majestic swan
With his mad gestures, foolish and sublime,
As of an exile whom one great desire
Gnaws with no truce. And then I thought of you,
Andromache! torn from your hero's arms;
Beneath the hand of Pyrrhus in his pride;

THE SWAN.

Bent o'er an empty tomb in ecstasy;
Widow of Hector — wife of Helenus!
And of the negress, wan and phthisical,
Tramping the mud, and with her haggard eyes
Seeking beyond the mighty walls of fog
The absent palm-trees of proud Africa;
Of all who lose that which they never find;
Of all who drink of tears; all whom grey grief
Gives suck to as the kindly wolf gave suck;
Of meagre orphans who like blossoms fade.
And one old Memory like a crying horn
Sounds through the forest where my soul is lost . . .
I think of sailors on some isle forgotten;
Of captives; vanquished . . . and of many more.

THE SEVEN OLD MEN.

O SWARMING city, city full of dreams,
Where in full day the spectre walks and speaks;
Mighty colossus, in your narrow veins
My story flows as flows the rising sap.

One morn. disputing with my tired soul.
And like a hero stiffening all my nerves,
I trod a suburb shaken by the jar
Of rolling wheels, where the fog magnified
The houses either side of that sad street,
So they seemed like two wharves the ebbing flood
Leaves desolate by the river-side. A mist,
Unclean and yellow, inundated space —
A scene that would have pleased an actor's soul.
Then suddenly an aged man, whose rags
Were yellow as the rainy sky, whose looks
Should have brought alms in floods upon his head,
Without the misery gleaming in his eye,
Appeared before me; and his pupils seemed
To have been washed with gall; the bitter frost
Sharpened his glance; and from his chin a beard
Sword-stiff and ragged, Judas-like stuck forth.
He was not bent but broken: his backbone

THE SEVEN OLD MEN.

Made a so true right angle with his legs,
That, as he walked, the tapping stick which gave
The finish to the picture, made him seem
Like some infirm and stumbling quadruped
Or a three-legged Jew.   Through snow and mud
He walked with troubled and uncertain gait,
As though his sabots trod upon the dead,
Indifferent and hostile to the world.

His double followed him: tatters and stick
And back and eye and beard, all were the same;
Out of the same Hell, indistinguishable,
These centenarian twins, these spectres odd,
Trod the same pace toward some end unknown.
To what fell complot was I then exposed?
Humiliated by what evil chance?
For as the minutes one by one went by
Seven times I saw this sinister old man
Repeat his image there before my eyes!

Let him who smiles at my inquietude,
Who never trembled at a fear like mine,
Know that in their decrepitude's despite
These seven old hideous monsters had the mien
Of beings immortal.

                          Then, I thought, must I,

THE SEVEN OLD MEN.

Undying, contemplate the awful eighth;
Inexorable, fatal, and ironic double;
Disgusting Phœnix, father of himself
And his own son? In terror then I turned
My back upon the infernal band, and fled
To my own place, and closed my door; distraught
And like a drunkard who sees all things twice,
With feverish troubled spirit, chilly and sick,
Wounded by mystery and absurdity!

In vain my reason tried to cross the bar,
The whirling storm but drove her back again;
And my soul tossed, and tossed, an outworn wreck,
Mastless, upon a monstrous, shoreless sea.

THE LITTLE OLD WOMEN.

Deep in the tortuous folds of ancient towns,
Where all, even horror, to enchantment turns,
I watch, obedient to my fatal mood,
For the decrepit, strange and charming beings,
The dislocated monsters that of old
Were lovely women — Laïs or Eponine!
Hunchbacked and broken, crooked though they be,
Let us still love them, for they still have souls.
They creep along wrapped in their chilly rags,
Beneath the whipping of the wicked wind,
They tremble when an omnibus rolls by,
And at their sides, a relic of the past,
A little flower-embroidered satchel hangs.
They trot about, most like to marionettes;
They drag themselves, as does a wounded beast;
Or dance unwillingly as a clapping bell
Where hangs and swings a demon without pity.
Though they be broken they have piercing eyes,
That shine like pools where water sleeps at night;
The astonished and divine eyes of a child
Who laughs at all that glitters in the world.

THE LITTLE OLD WOMEN.

Have you not seen that most old women's shrouds
Are little like the shroud of a dead child?
Wise Death, in token of his happy whim,
Wraps old and young in one enfolding sheet.
And when I see a phantom, frail and wan,
Traverse the swarming picture that is Paris,
It ever seems as though the delicate thing
Trod with soft steps towards a cradle new.
And then I wonder, seeing the twisted form,
How many times must workmen change the shape
Of boxes where at length such limbs are laid?
These eyes are wells brimmed with a million tears;
Crucibles where the cooling metal pales —
Mysterious eyes that are strong charms to him
Whose life-long nurse has been austere Disaster.

II.

The love-sick vestal of the old " Frasciti ";
Priestess of Thalia, alas! whose name
Only the prompter knows and he is dead;
Bygone celebrities that in bygone days
The Tivoli o'ershadowed in their bloom;
All charm me; yet among these beings frail
Three, turning pain to honey-sweetness, said
To the Devotion that had lent them wings:

THE LITTLE OLD WOMEN.

"Lift me, O powerful Hippogriffe, to the skies" —
One by her country to despair was driven;
One by her husband overwhelmed with grief;
One wounded by her child, Madonna-like;
Each could have made a river with her tears.

III.

Oft have I followed one of these old women,
One among others, when the falling sun
Reddened the heavens with a crimson wound —
Pensive, apart, she rested on a bench
To hear the brazen music of the band,
Played by the soldiers in the public park
To pour some courage into citizens' hearts,
On golden eves when all the world revives.
Proud and erect she drank the music in,
The lively and the warlike call to arms;
Her eyes blinked like an ancient eagle's eyes;
Her forehead seemed to await the laurel crown!

IV.

Thus you do wander, uncomplaining Stoics,
Through all the chaos of the living town:
Mothers with bleeding hearts, saints, courtesans,
Whose names of yore were on the lips of all;

THE LITTLE OLD WOMEN.

Who were all glory and all grace, and now
None know you; and the brutish drunkard stops,
Insulting you with his derisive love;
And cowardly urchins call behind your back.
Ashamed of living, withered shadows all,
With fear-bowed backs you creep beside the walls,
And none salute you, destined to loneliness!
Refuse of Time ripe for Eternity!
But I, who watch you tenderly afar,
With unquiet eyes on your uncertain steps,
As though I were your father, I — O wonder! —
Unknown to you taste secret, hidden joy.
I see your maiden passions bud and bloom,
Sombre or luminous, and your lost days
Unroll before me while my heart enjoys
All your old vices, and my soul expands
To all the virtues that have once been yours.
Ruined! and my sisters! O congenerate hearts,
Octogenarian Eves o'er whom is stretched
God's awful claw, where will you be to-morrow?

A MADRIGAL OF SORROW.

WHAT do I care though you be wise?
  Be sad, be beautiful; your tears
But add one more charm to your eyes,
As streams to valleys where they rise;
  And fairer every flower appears

After the storm. I love you most
  When joy has fled your brow downcast;
When your heart is in horror lost,
And o'er your present like a ghost
  Floats the dark shadow of the past.

I love you when the teardrop flows,
  Hotter than blood, from your large eye;
When I would hush you to repose
Your heavy pain breaks forth and grows
  Into a loud and tortured cry.

And then, voluptuousness divine!
  Delicious ritual and profound!
I drink in every sob like wine,
And dream that in your deep heart shine
  The pearls wherein your eyes were drowned.

A MADRIGAL OF SORROW.

I know your heart, which overflows
  With outworn loves long cast aside,
Still like a furnace flames and glows,
And you within your breast enclose
  A damnèd soul's unbending pride;

But till your dreams without release
  Reflect the leaping flames of hell;
Till in a nightmare without cease
You dream of poison to bring peace,
  And love cold steel and powder well;

And tremble at each opened door,
  And feel for every man distrust,
And shudder at the striking hour —
Till then you have not felt the power
  Of Irresistible Disgust.

My queen, my slave, whose love is fear,
  When you awaken shuddering,
Until that awful hour be here,
You cannot say at midnight drear:
  " I am your equal, O my King! "

THE IDEAL.

Not all the beauties in old prints vignetted,
  The worthless products of an outworn age,
With slippered feet and fingers castanetted,
  The thirst of hearts like this heart can assuage.

To Gavarni, the poet of chloroses,
  I leave his troupes of beauties sick and wan;
I cannot find among these pale, pale roses,
  The red ideal mine eyes would gaze upon.

Lady Macbeth, the lovely star of crime,
The Greek poet's dream born in a northern clime —
  Ah, she could quench my dark heart's deep desiring;

Or Michelangelo's dark daughter Night,
  In a strange posture dreamily admiring
Her beauty fashioned for a giant's delight!

MIST AND RAIN.

AUTUMNS and winters, springs of mire and rain,
Seasons of sleep, I sing your praises loud,
For thus I love to wrap my heart and brain
In some dim tomb beneath a vapoury shroud

In the wide plain where revels the cold wind,
Through long nights when the weathercock whirls
    round,
More free than in warm summer day my mind
Lifts wide her raven pinions from the ground.

Unto a heart filled with funereal things
That since old days hoar frosts have gathered on,
Naught is more sweet, O pallid, queenly springs,

Than the long pageant of your shadows wan,
Unless it be on moonless eves to weep
On some chance bed and rock our griefs to sleep.

SUNSET.

FAIR is the sun when first he flames above,
  Flinging his joy down in a happy beam;
And happy he who can salute with love
  The sunset far more glorious than a dream.

Flower, stream, and furrow! — I have seen them all
  In the sun's eye swoon like one trembling heart —
Though it be late let us with speed depart
  To catch at least one last ray ere it fall!

But I pursue the fading god in vain,
For conquering Night makes firm her dark domain,
  Mist and gloom fall, and terrors glide between,

And graveyard odours in the shadow swim,
And my faint footsteps on the marsh's rim,
  Bruise the cold snail and crawling toad unseen.

THE CORPSE.

REMEMBER, my Beloved, what thing we met
  By the roadside on that sweet summer day;
There on a grassy couch with pebbles set,
    A loathsome body lay.

The wanton limbs stiff-stretched into the air,
  Steaming with exhalations vile and dank,
In ruthless cynic fashion had laid bare
    The swollen side and flank.

On this decay the sun shone hot from heaven
  As though with chemic heat to broil and burn,
And unto Nature all that she had given
    A hundredfold return.

The sky smiled down upon the horror there
  As on a flower that opens to the day;
So awful an infection smote the air,
    Almost you swooned away.

The swarming flies hummed on the putrid side,
  Whence poured the maggots in a darkling stream,
That ran along these tatters of life's pride
    With a liquescent gleam.

THE CORPSE.

And like a wave the maggots rose and fell,
  The murmuring flies swirled round in busy strife:
It seemed as though a vague breath came to swell
  And multiply with life

The hideous corpse. From all this living world
  A music as of wind and water ran,
Or as of grain in rhythmic motion swirled
  By the swift winnower's fan.

And then the vague forms like a dream died out,
  Or like some distant scene that slowly falls
Upon the artist's canvas, that with doubt
  He only half recalls.

A homeless dog behind the boulders lay
  And watched us both with angry eyes forlorn,
Waiting a chance to come and take away
  The morsel she had torn.

        .   .   .   .

And you, even you, will be like this drear thing,
  A vile infection man may not endure;
Star that I yearn to! Sun that lights my spring!
  O passionate and pure!

THE CORPSE.

Yes, such will you be, Queen of every grace!
  When the last sacramental words are said;
And beneath grass and flowers that lovely face
  Moulders among the dead.

Then, O Belovèd, whisper to the worm
  That crawls up to devour you with a kiss,
That I still guard in memory the dear form
  Of love that comes to this!

AN ALLEGORY.

HERE is a woman, richly clad and fair,
Who in her wine dips her long, heavy hair;
Love's claws, and that sharp poison which is sin,
Are dulled against the granite of her skin.
Death she defies, Debauch she smiles upon,
For their sharp scythe-like talons every one
Pass by her in their all-destructive play;
Leaving her beauty till a later day.
Goddess she walks; sultana in her leisure;
She has Mohammed's faith that heaven is pleasure,
And bids all men forget the world's alarms
Upon her breast, between her open arms.
She knows, and she believes, this sterile maid,
Without whom the world's onward dream would fade,
That bodily beauty is the supreme gift
Which may from every sin the terror lift.
Hell she ignores, and Purgatory defies;
And when black Night shall roll before her eyes,
She will look straight in Death's grim face forlorn,
Without remorse or hate — as one new born.

THE ACCURSED.

Like pensive herds at rest upon the sands,
   These to the sea-horizons turn their eyes;
Out of their folded feet and clinging hands
   Bitter sharp tremblings and soft languors rise.

Some tread the thicket by the babbling stream,
   Their hearts with untold secrets ill at ease;
Calling the lover of their childhood's dream,
   They wound the green bark of the shooting trees.

Others like sisters wander, grave and slow,
   Among the rocks haunted by spectres thin,
Where Antony saw as larvæ surge and flow
   The veined bare breasts that tempted him to sin.

Some, when the resinous torch of burning wood
   Flares in lost pagan caverns dark and deep,
Call thee to quench the fever in their blood,
   Bacchus, who singest old remorse to sleep!

Then there are those the scapular bedights,
   Whose long white vestments hide the whip's red
      stain,
Who mix, in sombre woods on lonely nights,
   The foam of pleasure with the tears of pain.

THE ACCURSED.

O virgins, demons, monsters, martyrs! ye
　　Who scorn whatever actual appears;
Saints, satyrs. seekers of Infinity,
　　So full of cries, so full of bitter tears;

Ye whom my soul has followed into hell,
　　I love and pity, O sad sisters mine,
Your thirsts unquenched, your pains no tongue can
　　　　tell,
　　And your great hearts, those urns of love divine!

LA BEATRICE.

IN a burnt, ashen land, where no herb grew,
I to the winds my cries of anguish threw;
And in my thoughts, in that sad place apart,
Pricked gently with the poignard o'er my heart.
Then in full noon above my head a cloud
Descended tempest-swollen, and a crowd
Of wild, lascivious spirits huddled there,
The cruel and curious demons of the air,
Who coldly to consider me began;
Then, as a crowd jeers some unhappy man,
Exchanging gestures, winking with their eyes —
I heard a laughing and a whispering rise:

"Let us at leisure contemplate this clown,
This shadow of Hamlet aping Hamlet's frown,
With wandering eyes and hair upon the wind.
Is't not a pity that this empty mind,
This tramp, this actor out of work, this droll,
Because he knows how to assume a rôle
Should dream that eagles and insects, streams and
    woods,
Stand still to hear him chaunt his dolorous moods?

[65]

LA BEATRICE.

Even unto us, who made these ancient things,
The fool his public lamentation sings."

With pride as lofty as the towering cloud,
I would have stilled these clamouring demons loud,
And turned in scorn my sovereign head away
Had I not seen — O sight to dim the day! —
There in the middle of the troupe obscene
The proud and peerless beauty of my Queen!
She laughed with them at all my dark distress,
And gave to each in turn a vile caress.

THE SOUL OF WINE.

ONE eve in the bottle sang the soul of wine:
  "Man, unto thee, dear disinherited,
I sing a song of love and light divine —
  Prisoned in glass beneath my seals of red.

"I know thou labourest on the hill of fire,
  In sweat and pain beneath a flaming sun,
To give the life and soul my vines desire,
  And I am grateful for thy labours done.

"For I find joys unnumbered when I lave
  The throat of man by travail long outworn,
And his hot bosom is a sweeter grave
  Of sounder sleep than my cold caves forlorn.

"Hearest thou not the echoing Sabbath sound?
  The hope that whispers in my trembling breast?
Thy elbows on the table! gaze around;
  Glorify me with joy and be at rest.

"To thy wife's eyes I'll bring their long-lost gleam,
  I'll bring back to thy child his strength and light,
To him, life's fragile athlete I will seem
  Rare oil that firms his muscles for the fight.

THE SOUL OF WINE.

" I flow in man's heart as ambrosia flows;
  The grain the eternal Sower casts in the sod —
From our first loves the first fair verse arose,
  Flower-like aspiring to the heavens and God! "

THE WINE OF LOVERS.

SPACE rolls to-day her splendour round!
Unbridled, spurless, without bound,
Mount we upon the wings of wine
For skies fantastic and divine!

Let us, like angels tortured by
Some wild delirious phantasy,
Follow the far-off mirage born
In the blue crystal of the morn.

And gently balanced on the wing
Of the wild whirlwind we will ride,
Rejoicing with the joyous thing.

My sister, floating side by side,
Fly we unceasing whither gleams
The distant heaven of my dreams.

THE DEATH OF LOVERS.

THERE shall be couches whence faint odours rise,
  Divans like sepulchres, deep and profound;
Strange flowers that bloomed beneath diviner skies
  The death-bed of our love shall breathe around.

And guarding their last embers till the end,
  Our hearts shall be the torches of the shrine,
And their two leaping flames shall fade and blend
  In the twin mirrors of your soul and mine.

And through the eve of rose and mystic blue
A beam of love shall pass from me to you,
  Like a long sigh charged with a last farewell;

And later still an angel, flinging wide
The gates, shall bring to life with joyful spell
The tarnished mirrors and the flames that died.

THE DEATH OF THE POOR.

DEATH is consoler and Death brings to life;
  The end of all, the solitary hope;
We, drunk with Death's elixir, face the strife,
  Take heart, and mount till eve the weary slope.

Across the storm, the hoar-frost, and the snow,
  Death on our dark horizon pulses clear;
Death is the famous hostel we all know,
  Where we may rest and sleep and have good cheer.

Death is an angel whose magnetic palms
Bring dreams of ecstasy and slumberous calms
To smooth the beds of naked men and poor.

Death is the mystic granary of God;
The poor man's purse; his fatherland of yore;
The Gate that opens into heavens untrod!

THE BENEDICTION.

WHEN by the high decree of powers supreme,
   The Poet came into this world outworn,
She who had borne him, in a ghastly dream,
   Clenched blasphemous hands at God, and cried in
      scorn:

" O rather had I borne a writhing knot
   Of unclean vipers, than my breast should nurse
This vile derision, of my joy begot
   To be my expiation and my curse!

" Since of all women thou hast made of me
   Unto my husband a disgust and shame;
Since I may not cast this monstrosity,
   Like an old love-epistle, to the flame;

" I will pour out thine overwhelming hate
   On this the accursed weapon of thy spite;
This stunted tree I will so desecrate
   That not one tainted bud shall see the light! "

THE BENEDICTION.

So foaming with the foam of hate and shame,
  Blind unto God's design inexorable,
With her own hands she fed the purging flame
  To crimes maternal consecrate in hell.

Meanwhile beneath an Angel's care unseen
  The child disowned grows drunken with the sun;
His food and drink, though they be poor and mean,
  With streams of nectar and ambrosia run.

Speaking to clouds and playing with the wind,
  With joy he sings the sad Way of the Rood;
His shadowing pilgrim spirit weeps behind
  To see him gay as birds are in the wood.

Those he would love looked sideways and with fear,
  Or, taking courage from his aspect mild,
Sought who should first bring to his eye the tear,
  And spent their anger on the dreaming child.

With all the bread and wine the Poet must eat
  They mingled earth and ash and excrement,
All things he touched were spurned beneath their feet;
  They mourned if they must tread the road he went.

His wife ran crying in the public square:
  " Since he has found me worthy to adore,
Shall I not be as antique idols were,
  With gold and with bright colours painted o'er?

THE BENEDICTION.

" I will be drunk with nard and frankincense,
   With myrrh, and knees bowed down, and flesh and
      wine.
Can I not, smiling, in his love-sick sense,
   Usurp the homage due to beings divine?

" I will lay on him my fierce, fragile hand
   When I am weary of the impious play;
For well these harpy talons understand
   To furrow to his heart their crimson way.

" I'll tear the red thing beating from his breast,
   To cast it with disdain upon the ground,
Like a young bird torn trembling from the nest —
   His heart shall go to gorge my favourite hound."

To the far heaven, where gleams a splendid throne,
   The Poet uplifts his arms in calm delight,
And the vast beams from his pure spirit flown,
   Wrap all the furious peoples from his sight:

" Thou, O my God, be blest who givest pain,
   The balm divine for each imperfect heart,
The strong pure essence cleansing every stain
   Of sin that keeps us from thy joys apart.

THE BENEDICTION.

" Among the numbers of thy legions blest,
   I know a place awaits the poet there;
Him thou hast bid attend the eternal feast
   That Thrones and Virtues and Dominions share.

" I know the one thing noble is a grief
   Withstanding earth's and hell's destructive tooth,
And I, through all my dolorous life and brief,
   To gain the mystic crown, must cry the truth.

" The jewels lost in Palmyra of old,
   Metals unknown, pearls of the outer sea,
Are far too dim to set within the gold
   Of the bright crown that Time prepares for me.

" For it is wrought of pure unmingled light,
   Dipped in the white flame whence all flame is
      born —
The flame that makes all eyes, though diamond-bright,
   Seem obscure mirrors, darkened and forlorn."

GYPSIES TRAVELLING.

THE tribe prophetic with the eyes of fire
Went forth last night; their little ones at rest
Each on his mother's back, with his desire
Set on the ready treasure of her breast.

Laden with shining arms the men-folk tread
By the long wagons where their goods lie hidden;
They watch the heaven with eyes grown wearïed
Of hopeless dreams that come to them unbidden.

The grasshopper, from out his sandy screen,
Watching them pass redoubles his shrill song;
Dian, who loves them, makes the grass more green,

And makes the rock run water for this throng
Of ever-wandering ones whose calm eyes see
Familiar realms of darkness yet to be.

FRANCISCÆ MEÆ LAUDES.

Novis te cantabo chordis,
O novelletum quod ludis
In solitudine cordis.

Esto sertis implicata,
O fœmina delicata
Per quam solvuntur peccata!

Sicut beneficum Lethe,
Hauriam oscula de te,
Quæ imbuta es magnete.

Quum vitiorum tempestas
Turbabat omnes semitas,
Apparuisti, Deitas,

Velut stella salutaris
In naufragiis amaris . . .
Suspendam cor tuis aris!

Piscina plena virtutis,
Fons æternæ juventutis,
Labris vocem redde mutis!

FRANCISCÆ MEÆ LAUDES.

Quod erat spurcum, cremasti;
Quod rudius, exæquasti;
Quod debile, confirmasti!

In fame mea taberna,
In nocte mea lucerna,
Recte me semper guberna.

Adde nunc vires viribus,
Dulce balneum suavibus,
Unguentatum odoribus!

Meos circa lumbos mica,
O castitatis lorica,
Aqua tincta seraphica;

Patera gemmis corusca,
Panis salsus, mollis esca,
Divinum vinum, Francisca!

ROBED IN A SILKEN ROBE.

ROBED in a silken robe that shines and shakes,
  She seems to dance whene'er she treads the sod,
Like the long serpent that a fakir makes
  Dance to the waving cadence of a rod.

As the sad sand upon the desert's verge,
  Insensible to mortal grief and strife;
As the long weeds that float among the surge,
  She folds indifference round her budding life.

Her eyes are carved of minerals pure and cold,
And in her strange symbolic nature where
An angel mingles with the sphinx of old,

Where all is gold and steel and light and air,
For ever, like a vain star, unafraid
Shines the cold hauteur of the sterile maid.

A LANDSCAPE.

I WOULD, when I compose my solemn verse,
Sleep near the heaven as do astrologers,
Near the high bells, and with a dreaming mind
Hear their calm hymns blown to me on the wind.

Out of my tower, with chin upon my hands,
I'll watch the singing, babbling human bands;
And see clock-towers like spars against the sky,
And heavens that bring thoughts of eternity;

And softly, through the mist. will watch the birth
Of stars in heaven and lamplight on the earth;
The threads of smoke that rise above the town;
The moon that pours her pale enchantment down.

Seasons will pass till Autumn fades the rose;
And when comes Winter with his weary snows,
I'll shut the doors and window-casements tight,
And build my faery palace in the night.

Then I will dream of blue horizons deep;
Of gardens where the marble fountains weep;
Of kisses, and of ever-singing birds —
A sinless Idyll built of innocent words.

A LANDSCAPE.

And Trouble, knocking at my window-pane
And at my closet door, shall knock in vain;
I will not heed him with his stealthy tread,
Nor from my reverie uplift my head;

For I will plunge deep in the pleasure still
Of summoning the spring-time with my will,
Drawing the sun out of my heart. and there
With burning thoughts making a summer air.

THE VOYAGE.

THE world is equal to the child's desire
Who plays with pictures by his nursery fire—
How vast the world by lamplight seems! How small
When memory's eyes look back, remembering all!—

One morning we set forth with thoughts aflame,
Or heart o'erladen with desire or shame;
And cradle, to the song of surge and breeze,
Our own infinity on the finite seas.

Some flee the memory of their childhood's home;
And others flee their fatherland; and some,
Star-gazers drowned within a woman's eyes,
Flee from the tyrant Circe's witcheries;

And, lest they still be changed to beasts, take flight
For the embrasured heavens, and space, and light,
Till one by one the stains her kisses made
In biting cold and burning sunlight fade.

But the true voyagers are they who part
From all they love because a wandering heart
Drives them to fly the Fate they cannot fly;
Whose call is ever " On! "—they know not why.

THE VOYAGE.

Their thoughts are like the clouds that veil a star;
They dream of change as warriors dream of war;
And strange wild wishes never twice the same:
Desires no mortal man can give a name.

II.

We are like whirling tops and rolling balls —
For even when the sleepy night-time falls,
Old Curiosity still thrusts us on,
Like the cruel Angel who goads forth the sun.

The end of fate fades ever through the air,
And, being nowhere, may be anywhere
Where a man runs, hope waking in his breast,
For ever like a madman, seeking rest.

Our souls are wandering ships outweariëd;
And one upon the bridge asks: "What's ahead?"
The topman's voice with an exultant sound
Cries: "Love and Glory!" — then we run aground.

Each isle the pilot signals when 'tis late,
Is El Dorado, promised us by fate —
Imagination, spite of her belief,
Finds, in the light of dawn, a barren reef.

THE VOYAGE.

Oh the poor seeker after lands that flee!
Shall we not bind and cast into the sea
This drunken sailor whose ecstatic mood
Makes bitterer still the water's weary flood?

Such is an old tramp wandering in the mire,
Dreaming the paradise of his own desire,
Discovering cities of enchanted sleep
Where'er the light shines on a rubbish heap.

III.

Strange voyagers, what tales of noble deeds
Deep in your dim sea-weary eyes one reads!
Open the casket where your memories are,
And show each jewel, fashioned from a star;

For I would travel without sail or wind,
And so, to lift the sorrow from my mind,
Let your long memories of sea-days far fled
Pass o'er my spirit like a sail outspread.

What have you seen?

IV.

         "We have seen waves and stars,
And lost sea-beaches, and known many wars,
And notwithstanding war and hope and fear,
We were as weary there as we are here.

THE VOYAGE.

"The lights that on the violet sea poured down,
The suns that set behind some far-off town,
Lit in our hearts the unquiet wish to fly
Deep in the glimmering distance of the sky;

"The loveliest countries that rich cities bless,
Never contained the strange wild loveliness
By fate and chance shaped from the floating cloud —
And we were always sorrowful and proud!

"Desire from joy gains strength in weightier measure.
Desire, old tree who draw'st thy sap from pleasure,
Though thy bark thickens as the years pass by,
Thine arduous branches rise towards the sky;

"And wilt thou still grow taller, tree more fair
Than the tall cypress?
           — Thus have we, with care,
Gathered some flowers to please your eager mood,
Brothers who dream that distant things are good!

"We have seen many a jewel-glimmering throne;
And bowed to Idols when wild horns were blown
In palaces whose faery pomp and gleam
To your rich men would be a ruinous dream;

"And robes that were a madness to the eyes;
Women whose teeth and nails were stained with dyes;
Wise jugglers round whose neck the serpent winds — "

THE VOYAGE.

V.

And then, and then what more?

VI.

"O childish minds!

"Forget not that which we found everywhere,
From top to bottom of the fatal stair,
Above, beneath, around us and within,
The weary pageant of immortal sin.

"We have seen woman, stupid slave and proud,
Before her own frail, foolish beauty bowed;
And man, a greedy, cruel, lascivious fool,
Slave of the slave, a ripple in a pool;

"The martyrs groan, the headsman's merry mood;
And banquets seasoned and perfumed with blood;
Poison, that gives the tyrant's power the slip;
And nations amorous of the brutal whip;

"Many religions not unlike our own,
All in full flight for heaven's resplendent throne;
And Sanctity, seeking delight in pain,
Like a sick man of his own sickness vain;

THE VOYAGE.

" And mad mortality, drunk with its own power,
As foolish now as in a bygone hour,
Shouting, in presence of the tortured Christ:
' I curse thee, mine own Image sacrificed.'

" And silly monks in love with Lunacy,
Fleeing the troops herded by destiny,
Who seek for peace in opiate slumber furled —
Such is the pageant of the rolling world! "

VII.

O bitter knowledge that the wanderers gain!
The world says our own age is little and vain;
For ever, yesterday, to-day, to-morrow,
'Tis horror's oasis in the sands of sorrow.

Must we depart? If you can rest, remain;
Part, if you must. Some fly, some cower in vain,
Hoping that Time, the grim and eager foe,
Will pass them by; and some run to and fro

Like the Apostles or the Wandering Jew;
Go where they will, the Slayer goes there too!
And there are some, and these are of the wise,
Who die as soon as birth has lit their eyes.

THE VOYAGE.

But when at length the Slayer treads us low,
We will have hope and cry, " 'Tis time to go! "
As when of old we parted for Cathay
With wind-blown hair and eyes upon the bay.

We will embark upon the Shadowy Sea,
Like youthful wanderers for the first time free —
Hear you the lovely and funereal voice
That sings: *O come all ye whose wandering joys*
Are set upon the scented Lotus flower,
For here we sell the fruit's miraculous boon;
Come ye and drink the sweet and sleepy power
Of the enchanted, endless afternoon.

VIII.

O Death, old Captain, it is time, put forth!
We have grown weary of the gloomy north;
Though sea and sky are black as ink, lift sail!
Our hearts are full of light and will not fail.

O pour thy sleepy poison in the cup!
The fire within the heart so burns us up
That we would wander Hell and Heaven through,
Deep in the Unknown seeking something *new!*

LITTLE POEMS IN PROSE

THE STRANGER.

TELL me, enigmatic man, whom do you love best? Your father, your mother, your sister, or your brother?

"I have neither father, nor mother, nor sister, nor brother."

Your friends, then?

"You use a word that until now has had no meaning for me."

Your country?

"I am ignorant of the latitude in which it is situated."

Then Beauty?

"Her I would love willingly, goddess and immortal."

Gold?

"I hate it as you hate your God."

What, then, extraordinary stranger, do you love?

"I love the clouds — the clouds that pass — yonder — the marvellous clouds."

EVERY MAN HIS CHIMÆRA.

BENEATH a broad grey sky, upon a vast and dusty plain devoid of grass, and where not even a nettle or a thistle was to be seen, I met several men who walked bowed down to the ground.

Each one carried upon his back an enormous Chimæra as heavy as a sack of flour or coal, or as the equipment of a Roman foot-soldier.

But the monstrous beast was not a dead weight, rather she enveloped and oppressed the men with her powerful and elastic muscles, and clawed with her two vast talons at the breast of her mount. Her fabulous head reposed upon the brow of the man like one of those horrible casques by which ancient warriors hoped to add to the terrors of the enemy.

I questioned one of the men, asking him why they went so. He replied that he knew nothing, neither he nor the others, but that evidently they went somewhere, since they were urged on by an unconquerable desire to walk.

Very curiously, none of the wayfarers seemed to be irritated by the ferocious beast hanging at his neck

[92]

and cleaving to his back: one had said that he considered it as a part of himself. These grave and weary faces bore witness to no despair. Beneath the splenetic cupola of the heavens, their feet trudging through the dust of an earth as desolate as the sky, they journeyed onwards with the resigned faces of men condemned to hope for ever. So the train passed me and faded into the atmosphere of the horizon at the place where the planet unveils herself to the curiosity of the human eye.

During several moments I obstinately endeavoured to comprehend this mystery; but irresistible Indifference soon threw herself upon me, nor was I more heavily dejected thereby than they by their crushing Chimæras.

VENUS AND THE FOOL.

How admirable the day! The vast park swoons beneath the burning eye of the sun, as youth beneath the lordship of love.

There is no rumour of the universal ecstasy of all things. The waters themselves are as though drifting into sleep. Very different from the festivals of humanity, here is a silent revel.

It seems as though an ever-waning light makes all objects glimmer more and more, as though the excited flowers burn with a desire to rival the blue of the sky by the vividness of their colours; as though the heat, making perfumes visible, drives them in vapour towards their star.

Yet, in the midst of this universal joy, I have perceived one afflicted thing.

At the feet of a colossal Venus. one of those motley fools, those willing clowns whose business it is to bring laughter upon kings when weariness or remorse possesses them, lies wrapped in his gaudy and ridiculous garments, coiffed with his cap and bells, huddled against the pedestal, and raises towards the goddess his eyes filled with tears.

And his eyes say: "I am the last and most alone of all mortals, inferior to the meanest of animals in that I am denied either love or friendship. Yet I am made, even I, for the understanding and enjoyment of immortal Beauty. O Goddess, have pity upon my sadness and my frenzy."

The implacable Venus gazed into I know not what distances with her marble eyes.

INTOXICATION.

ONE must be for ever drunken: that is the sole question of importance. If you would not feel the horrible burden of Time that bruises your shoulders and bends you to the earth, you must be drunken without cease. But how? With wine, with poetry, with virtue, with what you please. But be drunken. And if sometimes, on the steps of a palace, on the green grass by a moat, or in the dull loneliness of your chamber, you should waken up, your intoxication already lessened or gone, ask of the wind, of the wave, of the star, of the bird, of the timepiece; ask of all that flees, all that sighs, all that revolves, all that sings, all that speaks, ask of these the hour; and wind and wave and star and bird and timepiece will answer you: " It is the hour to be drunken! Lest you be the martyred slaves of Time, intoxicate yourselves, be drunken without cease! With wine, with poetry, with virtue, or with what you will."

THE GIFTS OF THE MOON.

THE Moon, who is caprice itself, looked in' at the window as you slept in your cradle, and said to herself: "I am well pleased with this child."

And she softly descended her stairway of clouds and passed through the window-pane without noise. She bent over you with the supple tenderness of a mother and laid her colours upon your face. Therefrom your eyes have remained green and your cheeks extraordinarily pale. From contemplation of your visitor your eyes are so strangely wide; and she so tenderly wounded you upon the breast that you have ever kept a certain readiness to tears.

In the amplitude of her joy, the Moon filled all your chamber as with a phosphorescent air, a luminous poison; and all this living radiance thought and said: "You shall be for ever under the influence of my kiss. You shall love all that loves me and that I love: clouds, and silence, and night; the vast green sea; the unformed and multitudinous waters; the place where you are not; the lover you will never know; monstrous flowers, and perfumes that bring madness; cats that stretch themselves swooning upon the piano and lament with the sweet, hoarse voices of women.

" And you shall be loved of my lovers, courted of my courtesans. You shall be the Queen of men with green eyes, whose breasts also I have wounded in my nocturnal caress: men that love the sea, the immense green ungovernable sea; the unformed and multitudinous waters; the place where they are not; the woman they will never know; sinister flowers that seem to bear the incense of some unknown religion; perfumes that trouble the will; and all savage and voluptuous animals, images of their own folly."

And that is why I am couched at your feet, O spoiled child, beloved and accursed, seeking in all your being the reflection of that august divinity, that prophetic godmother, that poisonous nurse of all *lunatics.*

THE INVITATION TO THE VOYAGE.

IT is a superb land, a country of Cockaigne, as they say, that I dream of visiting with an old friend. A strange land, drowned in our northern fogs, that one might call the East of the West, the China of Europe; a land patiently and luxuriously decorated with the wise, delicate vegetations of a warm and capricious phantasy.

A true land of Cockaigne, where all is beautiful, rich, tranquil, and honest; where luxury is pleased to mirror itself in order; where life is opulent, and sweet to breathe; from whence disorder, turbulence, and the unforeseen are excluded; where happiness is married to silence; where even the food is poetic, rich and exciting at the same time; where all things, my beloved, are like you.

Do you know that feverish malady that seizes hold of us in our cold miseries; that nostalgia of a land unknown; that anguish of curiosity? It is a land which resembles you, where all is beautiful, rich, tranquil and honest, where phantasy has built and decorated an occidental China, where life is sweet to

[99]

THE INVITATION TO THE VOYAGE.

breathe, and happiness married to silence. It is there that one would live; there that one would die.

Yes, it is there that one must go to breathe, to dream, and to lengthen one's hours by an infinity of sensations. A musician has written the "Invitation to the Waltz"; where is he who will write the "Invitation to the Voyage," that one may offer it to his beloved, to the sister of his election?

Yes, it is in this atmosphere that it would be good to live, — yonder, where slower hours contain more thoughts, where the clocks strike the hours of happiness with a more profound and significant solemnity.

Upon the shining panels, or upon skins gilded with a sombre opulence, beatified paintings have a discreet life, as calm and profound as the souls of the artists who created them.

The setting suns that colour the rooms and salons with so rich a light, shine through veils of rich tapestry, or through high leaden-worked windows of many compartments. The furniture is massive, curious, and bizarre, armed with locks and secrets, like profound and refined souls. The mirrors, the metals, the silverwork and the china, play a mute and mysterious symphony for the eyes; and from all things, from the corners, from the chinks in the drawers, from the folds of drapery, a singular perfume escapes, a

THE INVITATION TO THE VOYAGE.

Sumatran *revenez-y*, which is like the soul of the apartment.

A true country of Cockaigne, I have said; where all is rich, correct and shining, like a beautiful conscience, or a splendid set of silver, or a medley of jewels. The treasures of the world flow there, as in the house of a laborious man who has well merited the entire world. A singular land, as superior to others as Art is superior to Nature; where Nature is made over again by dream; where she is corrected, embellished, refashioned.

Let them seek and seek again, let them extend the limits of their happiness for ever, these alchemists who work with flowers! Let them offer a prize of sixty or a hundred thousand florins to whosoever can solve their ambitious problems! As for me, I have found my *black tulip* and my *blue dahlia!*

Incomparable flower, tulip found at last, symbolical dahlia, it is there, is it not, in this so calm and dreamy land that you live and blossom? Will you not there be framed in your proper analogy, and will you not be mirrored, to speak like the mystics, in your own *correspondence?*

Dreams! — always dreams! and the more ambitious and delicate the soul, the farther from possibility is the dream. Every man carries within him his dose of natural opium, incessantly secreted and renewed, and, from birth to death. how many hours can we count that have been filled with positive joy, with successful and decided action?   Shall we ever live in and become a part of the picture my spirit has painted, the picture that resembles you?

These treasures, furnishings, luxury, order, perfumes and miraculous flowers, are you. You again are the great rivers and calm canals. The enormous ships drifting beneath their loads of riches, and musical with the sailors' monotonous song, are my thoughts that sleep and stir upon your breast. You take them gently to the sea that is Infinity, reflecting the profundities of the sky in the limpid waters of your lovely soul; — and when, outworn by the surge and gorged with the products of the Orient, the ships come back to the ports of home, they are still my thoughts, grown rich, that have returned to you from Infinity.

WHAT IS TRUTH?

I once knew a certain Benedicta whose presence filled the air with the ideal and whose eyes spread abroad the desire of grandeur, of beauty, of glory, and of all that makes man believe in immortality.

But this miraculous maiden was too beautiful for long life, so she died soon after I knew her first, and it was I myself who entombed her, upon a day when spring swung her censer even in the burial-ground. It was I myself who entombed her, fast closed in a coffin of perfumed wood, as uncorruptible as the coffers of India.

And, as my eyes rested upon the spot where my treasure lay hidden, I became suddenly aware of a little being who singularly resembled the dead; and who, stamping the newly-turned earth with a curious and hysterical violence, burst into laughter, and said: " It is I, the true Benedicta! It is I, the notorious drab! As the punishment of your folly and blindness you shall love me as I truly am."

But I, furious, replied: " No! " The better to emphasise my refusal I struck the ground so violently with my foot that my leg was thrust up to the knee in the recent grave, and I, like a wolf in a trap, was caught perhaps for ever in the Grave of the Ideal.

ALREADY!

A HUNDRED times already the sun had leaped, radiant or saddened, from the immense cup of the sea whose rim could scarcely be seen; a hundred times it had again sunk, glittering or morose, into its mighty bath of twilight. For many days we had contemplated the other side of the firmament, and deciphered the celestial alphabet of the antipodes. And each of the passengers sighed and complained. One had said that the approach of land only exasperated their sufferings. "When, then," they said, "shall we cease to sleep a sleep broken by the surge, troubled by a wind that snores louder than we? When shall we be able to eat at an unmoving table?"

There were those who thought of their own firesides, who regretted their sullen, faithless wives, and their noisy progeny. All so doted upon the image of the absent land, that I believe they would have eaten grass with as much enthusiasm as the beasts.

At length a coast was signalled, and on approaching we saw a magnificent and dazzling land. It seemed as though the music of life flowed therefrom in a vague murmur; and the banks, rich with all kinds of growths, breathed, for leagues around, a delicious odour of flowers and fruits.

Each one therefore was joyful; his evil humour left him. Quarrels were forgotten, reciprocal wrongs forgiven, the thought of duels was blotted out of the memory, and rancour fled away like smoke.

I alone was sad, inconceivably sad. Like a priest from whom one has torn his divinity, I could not, without heartbreaking bitterness, leave this so monstrously seductive ocean, this sea so infinitely various in its terrifying simplicity, which seemed to contain in itself and represent by its joys, and attractions, and angers, and smiles, the moods and agonies and ecstasies of all souls that have lived, that live, and that shall yet live.

In saying good-bye to this incomparable beauty I felt as though I had been smitten to death; and that is why when each of my companions said: "At last! " I could only cry "*Already!*"

Here meanwhile was the land, the land with its noises, its passions, its commodities, its festivals: a land rich and magnificent, full of promises, that sent to us a mysterious perfume of rose and musk, and from whence the music of life flowed in an amorous murmuring.

THE DOUBLE CHAMBER.

A CHAMBER that is like a reverie; a chamber truly *spiritual*, where the stagnant atmosphere is lightly touched with rose and blue.

There the soul bathes itself in indolence made odorous with regret and desire. There is some sense of the twilight, of things tinged with blue and rose: a dream of delight during an eclipse. The shape of the furniture is elongated, low, languishing; one would think it endowed with the somnambulistic vitality of plants and minerals.

The tapestries speak an inarticulate language, like the flowers, the skies, the dropping suns.

There are no artistic abominations upon the walls. Compared with the pure dream, with an impression unanalysed, definite art, positive art, is a blasphemy. Here all has the sufficing lucidity and the delicious obscurity of music.

An infinitesimal odour of the most exquisite choice, mingled with a floating humidity, swims in this atmosphere where the drowsing spirit is lulled by the sensations one feels in a hothouse.

The abundant muslin flows before the windows and

THE DOUBLE CHAMBER.

the couch, and spreads out in snowy cascades. Upon the couch lies the Idol, ruler of my dreams. But why is she here? — who has brought her? — what magical power has installed her upon this throne of delight and reverie? What matter — she is there; and I recognise her.

These indeed are the eyes whose flame pierces the twilight; the subtle and terrible mirrors that I recognise by their horrifying malice. They attract, they dominate, they devour the sight of whomsoever is imprudent enough to look at them. I have often studied them: these Black Stars that compel curiosity and admiration.

To what benevolent demon, then, do I owe being thus surrounded with mystery, with silence, with peace, and sweet odours? O beatitude! the thing we name life, even in its most fortunate amplitude, has nothing in common with this supreme life with which I am now acquainted, which I taste minute by minute, second by second.

Not so! Minutes are no more; seconds are no more. Time has vanished, and Eternity reigns — an Eternity of delight.

A heavy and terrible knocking reverberates upon the door, and, as in a hellish dream, it seems to me as though I had received a blow from a mattock.

THE DOUBLE CHAMBER.

Then a Spectre enters: it is an usher who comes to torture me in the name of the Law; an infamous concubine who comes to cry misery and to add the trivialities of her life to the sorrow of mine; or it may be the errand-boy of an editor who comes to implore the remainder of a manuscript.

The chamber of paradise, the Idol, the ruler of dreams, the Sylphide, as the great René said; all this magic has vanished at the brutal knocking of the Spectre.

Horror; I remember, I remember! Yes, this kennel, this habitation of eternal weariness, is indeed my own. Here is my senseless furniture, dusty and tattered; the dirty fireplace without a flame or an ember; the sad windows where the raindrops have traced runnels in the dust; the manuscripts, erased or unfinished; the almanac with the sinister days marked off with a pencil!

And this perfume of another world, whereof I intoxicated myself with a so perfected sensitiveness; alas, its place is taken by an odour of stale tobacco smoke, mingled with I know not what nauseating mustiness. Now one breathes here the rankness of desolation.

In this narrow world, narrow and yet full of disgust, a single familiar object smiles at me: the phial

THE DOUBLE CHAMBER.

of laudanum: old and terrible love; like all loves, alas! fruitful in caresses and treacheries.

Yes, Time has reappeared; Time reigns a monarch now: and with the hideous Ancient has returned all his demoniacal following of Memories, Regrets, Tremors, Fears, Dolours, Nightmares, and twittering nerves.

I assure you that the seconds are strongly and solemnly accentuated now; and each, as it drips from the pendulum, says: "I am Life: intolerable, implacable Life!"

There is not a second in mortal life whose mission it is to bear good news: the good news that brings the inexplicable tear to the eye.

Yes, Time reigns; Time has regained his brutal mastery. And he goads me, as though I were a steer, with his double goad: "Woa, thou fool! Sweat, then, thou slave! Live on, thou damnèd!"

AT ONE O'CLOCK IN THE MORNING.

ALONE at last! Nothing is to be heard but the rattle of a few tardy and tired-out cabs. There will be silence now, if not repose, for several hours at least. At last the tyranny of the human face has disappeared — I shall not suffer except alone. At last it is permitted me to refresh myself in a bath of shadows. But first a double turn of the key in the lock. It seems to me that this turn of the key will deepen my solitude and strengthen the barriers which actually separate me from the world.

A horrible life and a horrible city! Let us run over the events of the day. I have seen several literary men; one of them wished to know if he could get to Russia by land (he seemed to have an idea that Russia was an island); I have disputed generously enough with the editor of a review, who to each objection replied: "We take the part of respectable people," which implies that every other paper but his own is edited by a knave; I have saluted some twenty people, fifteen of them unknown to me; and shaken hands with a like number, without having taken the precaution of first buying gloves; I have been driven to kill time, during a shower, with a mountebank, who wanted me to design for her a costume as Venusta; I have made my bow to a theatre manager, who said: " You will do well, perhaps, to interview Z; he is the heaviest, foolishest, and most celebrated of all my authors; with him perhaps you will be able to come to something. See him, and then we'll see." I have boasted (why?) of several villainous deeds I never committed, and indignantly denied certain shameful things I accomplished with joy, certain misdeeds of fanfaronade, crimes of human respect; I have refused an easy favour to a friend and given a written recommendation to a perfect fool. Heavens! it's well ended.

Discontented with myself and with everything and everybody else, I should be glad enough to redeem myself and regain my self-respect in the silence and solitude.

Souls of those whom I have loved, whom I have sung, fortify me; sustain me; drive away the lies and the corrupting vapours of this world; and Thou, Lord my God, accord me so much grace as shall produce some beautiful verse to prove to myself that I am not the last of men, that I am not inferior to those I despise.

THE CONFITEOR OF THE ARTIST.

How penetrating is the end of an autumn day! Ah,
yes, penetrating enough to be painful even; for there
are certain delicious sensations whose vagueness does
not prevent them from being intense; and none more
keen than the perception of the Infinite. He has a
great delight who drowns his gaze in the immensity
of sky and sea. Solitude, silence, the incomparable
chastity of the azure — a little sail trembling upon
the horizon, by its very littleness and isolation imi-
tating my irremediable existence — the melodious
monotone of the surge — all these things thinking
through me and I through them (for in the grandeur
of the reverie the Ego is swiftly lost); they think,
I say, but musically and picturesquely, without quib-
bles, without syllogisms, without deductions.

These thoughts, as they arise in me or spring forth
from external objects, soon become always too in-
tense. The energy working within pleasure creates
an uneasiness, a positive suffering. My nerves are
too tense to give other than clamouring and dolorous
vibrations.

THE CONFITEOR OF THE ARTIST.

And now the profundity of the sky dismays me! its limpidity exasperates me. The insensibility of the sea, the immutability of the spectacle, revolt me. Ah, must one eternally suffer, for ever be a fugitive from Beauty?

Nature, pitiless enchantress, ever-victorious rival, leave me! Tempt my desires and my pride no more. The contemplation of Beauty is a duel where the artist screams with terror before being vanquished.

THE THYRSUS.

TO FRANZ LISZT.

WHAT is a thyrsus? According to the moral and poetical sense, it is a sacerdotal emblem in the hand of the priests or priestesses celebrating the divinity of whom they are the interpreters and servants. But physically it is no more than a baton, a pure staff, a hop-pole, a vine-prop; dry, straight, and hard. Around this baton, in capricious meanderings, stems and flowers twine and wanton; these, sinuous and fugitive; those, hanging like bells or inverted cups. And an astonishing complexity disengages itself from this complexity of tender or brilliant lines and colours. Would not one suppose that the curved line and the spiral pay their court to the straight line, and twine about it in a mute adoration? Would not one say that all these delicate corollæ, all these calices, explosions of odours and colours, execute a mystical dance around the hieratic staff? And what imprudent mortal will dare to decide whether the flowers and the vine branches have been made for the baton, or whether the baton is not but a pretext to set forth the beauty of the vine branches and the flowers?

THE THYRSUS.

The thyrsus is the symbol of your astonishing duality, O powerful and venerated master, dear bacchanal of a mysterious and impassioned Beauty. Never a nymph excited by the mysterious Dionysius shook her thyrsus over the heads of her companions with as much energy as your genius trembles in the hearts of your brothers. The baton is your will: erect, firm, unshakeable; the flowers are the wanderings of your fancy around it: the feminine element encircling the masculine with her illusive dance. Straight line and arabesque — intention and expression — the rigidity of the will and the suppleness of the word — a variety of means united for a single purpose — the all-powerful and indivisible amalgam that is genius — what analyst will have the detestable courage to divide or to separate you?

Dear Liszt, across the fogs, beyond the flowers, in towns where the pianos chant your glory, where the printing-house translates your wisdom; in whatever place you be, in the splendour of the Eternal City or among the fogs of the dreamy towns that Cambrinus consoles; improvising rituals of delight or ineffable pain, or giving to paper your abstruse meditations; singer of eternal pleasure and pain, philosopher, poet, and artist, I offer you the salutation of immortality!

THE MARKSMAN.

As the carriage traversed the wood he bade the driver draw up in the neighbourhood of a shooting gallery, saying that he would like to have a few shots to kill time. Is not the slaying of the monster Time the most ordinary and legitimate occupation of man? — So he gallantly offered his hand to his dear, adorable, and execrable wife; the mysterious woman to whom he owed so many pleasures, so many pains, and perhaps also a great part of his genius.

Several bullets went wide of the proposed mark, one of them flew far into the heavens, and as the charming creature laughed deliriously, mocking the clumsiness of her husband, he turned to her brusquely and said: "Observe that doll yonder, to the right, with its nose in the air, and with so haughty an appearance. Very well, dear angel, *I will imagine to myself that it is you!*"

He closed both eyes and pulled the trigger. The doll was neatly decapitated.

Then, bending towards his dear, adorable, and execrable wife, his inevitable and pitiless muse, he kissed her respectfully upon the hand, and added, "Ah, dear angel, how I thank you for my skill!"

[116]

THE SHOOTING-RANGE AND THE CEMETERY.

" CEMETERY View Inn " — " A queer sign," said our traveller to himself; " but it raises a thirst! Certainly the keeper of this inn appreciates Horace and the poet pupils of Epicurus. Perhaps he even apprehends the profound philosophy of those old Egyptians who had no feast without its skeleton, or some emblem of life's brevity."

He entered: drank a glass of beer in presence of the tombs; and slowly smoked a cigar. Then, his phantasy driving him, he went down into the cemetery, where the grass was so tall and inviting; so brilliant in the sunshine.

The light and heat, indeed, were so furiously intense that one had said the drunken sun wallowed upon a carpet of flowers that had fattened upon the corruption beneath.

The air was heavy with vivid rumours of life — the life of things infinitely small — and broken at intervals by the crackling of shots from a neighbouring shooting-range, that exploded with a sound as of champagne corks to the burden of a hollow symphony.

And then, beneath a sun which scorched the brain, and in that atmosphere charged with the ardent perfume of death, he heard a voice whispering out of the tomb where he sat. And this voice said: " Accursed be your rifles and targets, you turbulent living ones, who care so little for the dead in their divine repose! Accursed be your ambitions and calculations, importunate mortals who study the arts of slaughter near the sanctuary of Death himself! Did you but know how easy the prize to win, how facile the end to reach, and how all save Death is naught, not so greatly would you fatigue yourselves, O ye laborious alive; nor would you so often vex the slumber of them that long ago reached the End — the only true end of life detestable! "

THE DESIRE TO PAINT.

UNHAPPY perhaps is the man, but happy the artist, who is torn with this desire.

I burn to paint a certain woman who has appeared to me so rarely, and so swiftly fled away, like some beautiful, regrettable thing the traveller must leave behind him in the night. It is already long since I saw her.

She is beautiful, and more than beautiful: she is overpowering. The colour black preponderates in her; all that she inspires is nocturnal and profound. Her eyes are two caverns where mystery vaguely stirs and gleams; her glance illuminates like a ray of light; it is an explosion in the darkness.

I would compare her to a black sun if one could conceive of a dark star overthrowing light and happiness. But it is the moon that she makes one dream of most readily; the moon, who has without doubt touched her with her own influence; not the white moon of the idylls, who resembles a cold bride, but the sinister and intoxicating moon suspended in the depths of a stormy night, among the driven clouds;

THE DESIRE TO PAINT.

not the discreet peaceful moon who visits the dreams of pure men, but the moon torn from the sky, conquered and revolted, that the witches of Thessaly hardly constrain to dance upon the terrified grass.

Her small brow is the habitation of a tenacious will and the love of prey. And below this inquiet face, whose mobile nostrils breathe in the unknown and the impossible, glitters, with an unspeakable grace, the smile of a large mouth; white, red, and delicious; a mouth that makes one dream of the miracle of some superb flower unclosing in a volcanic land.

There are women who inspire one with the desire to woo them and win them; but she makes one wish to die slowly beneath her steady gaze.

THE GLASS-VENDOR.

THERE are some natures purely contemplative and antipathetic to action, who nevertheless, under a mysterious and inexplicable impulse, sometimes act with a rapidity of which they would have believed themselves incapable. Such a one is he who, fearing to find some new vexation awaiting him at his lodgings, prowls about in a cowardly fashion before the door without daring to enter; such a one is he who keeps a letter fifteen days without opening it, or only makes up his mind at the end of six months to undertake a journey that has been a necessity for a year past. Such beings sometimes feel themselves precipitately thrust towards action, like an arrow from a bow.

The novelist and the physician, who profess to know all things, yet cannot explain whence comes this sudden and delirious energy to indolent and voluptuous souls; nor how, incapable of accomplishing the simplest and most necessary things, they are at some certain moment of time possessed by a superabundant hardihood which enables them to execute the most absurd and even the most dangerous acts.

THE GLASS-VENDOR.

One of my friends, the most harmless dreamer that ever lived, at one time set fire to a forest, in order to ascertain, as he said, whether the flames take hold with the easiness that is commonly affirmed. His experiment failed ten times running, on the eleventh it succeeded only too well.

Another lit a cigar by the side of a powder barrel, *in order to see, to know, to tempt Destiny*, for a jest, to have the pleasure of suspense, for no reason at all, out of caprice, out of idleness. This is a kind of energy that springs from weariness and reverie; and those in whom it manifests so stubbornly are in general, as I have said, the most indolent and dreamy beings.

Another so timid that he must cast down his eyes before the gaze of any man, and summon all his poor will before he dare enter a café or pass the pay-box of a theatre, where the ticket-seller seems, in his eyes, invested with all the majesty of Minos, Æcus, and Rhadamanthus, will at times throw himself upon the neck of some old man whom he sees in the street, and embrace him with enthusiasm in sight of an astonished crowd. Why? Because — because this countenance is irresistibly attractive to him? Perhaps: but it is more legitimate to suppose that he himself does not know why.

THE GLASS-VENDOR.

I have been more than once a victim to these crises and outbreaks which give us cause to believe that evil-meaning demons slip into us, to make us the ignorant accomplices of their most absurd desires. One morning I arose in a sullen mood, very sad, and tired of idleness, and thrust as it seemed to me to the doing of some great thing, some brilliant act — and then, alas, I opened the window.

(I beg you to observe that in some people the spirit of mystification is not the result of labour or combination, but rather of a fortuitous inspiration which would partake, were it not for the strength of the feeling, of the mood called hysterical by the physician and satanic by those who think a little more profoundly than the physician; the mood which thrusts us unresisting to a multitude of dangerous and inconvenient acts.)

The first person I noticed in the street was a glass-vendor whose shrill and discordant cry mounted up to me through the heavy, dull atmosphere of Paris. It would have been else impossible to account for the sudden and despotic hatred of this poor man that came upon me.

"Hello, there!" I cried, and bade him ascend. Meanwhile I reflected, not without gaiety, that as my room was on the sixth landing, and the stairway very narrow, the man would have some difficulty in ascending, and in many a place would break off the corners of his fragile merchandise.

At length he appeared. I examined all his glasses with curiosity, and then said to him: " What, have you no coloured glasses? Glasses of rose and crimson and blue, magical glasses, glasses of Paradise? You are insolent. You dare to walk in mean streets when you have no glasses that would make one see beauty in life?" And I hurried him briskly to the staircase, which he staggered down, grumbling.

I went on to the balcony and caught up a little flower-pot, and when the man appeared in the doorway beneath I let fall my engine of war perpendicularly upon the edge of his pack, so that it was upset by the shock and all his poor walking fortune broken to bits. It made a noise like a palace of crystal shattered by lightning. Mad with my folly, I cried furiously after him: " The life beautiful! the life beautiful! "

Such nervous pleasantries are not without peril; often enough one pays dearly for them. But what matters an eternity of damnation to him who has found in one second an eternity of enjoyment?

THE WIDOWS.

VAUVENARGUES says that in public gardens there are alleys haunted principally by thwarted ambition, by unfortunate inventors, by aborted glories and broken hearts, and by all those tumultuous and contracted souls in whom the last sighs of the storm mutter yet again, and who thus betake themselves far from the insolent and joyous eyes of the well-to-do. These shadowy retreats are the rendezvous of life's cripples.

To such places above all others do the poet and philosopher direct their avid conjectures. They find there an unfailing pasturage, for if there is one place they disdain to visit it is, as I have already hinted, the place of the joy of the rich. A turmoil in the void has no attractions for them. On the contrary they feel themselves irresistibly drawn towards all that is feeble, ruined, sorrowing, and bereft.

An experienced eye is never deceived. In these rigid and dejected lineaments; in these eyes, wan and hollow, or bright with the last fading gleams of the combat against fate; in these numerous profound wrinkles and in the slow and troubled gait, the eye of experience deciphers unnumbered legends of mis-

THE WIDOWS.

taken devotion, of unrewarded effort, of hunger and cold humbly and silently supported.

Have you not at times seen widows sitting on the deserted benches? Poor widows, I mean. Whether in mourning or not they are easily recognised. Moreover, there is always something wanting in the mourning of the poor; a lack of harmony which but renders it the more heart-breaking. It is forced to be niggardly in its show of grief. They are the rich who exhibit a full complement of sorrow.

Who is the saddest and most saddening of widows: she who leads by the hand a child who cannot share her reveries, or she who is quite alone? I do not know. . . . It happened that I once followed for several long hours an aged and afflicted woman of this kind: rigid and erect, wrapped in a little worn shawl, she carried in all her being the pride of stoicism.

She was evidently condemned by her absolute loneliness to the habits of an ancient celibacy; and the masculine characters of her habits added to their austerity a piquant mysteriousness. In what miserable café she dines I know not, nor in what manner. I followed her to a reading-room, and for a long time watched her reading the papers, her active eyes, that once burned with tears, seeking for news of a powerful and personal interest.

THE WIDOWS.

At length, in the afternoon, under a charming autumnal sky, one of those skies that let fall hosts of memories and regrets, she seated herself remotely in a garden, to listen, far from the crowd, to one of the regimental bands whose music gratifies the people of Paris. This was without doubt the small debauch of the innocent old woman (or the purified old woman), the well-earned consolation for another of the burdensome days without a friend, without conversation, without joy, without a confidant, that God had allowed to fall upon her perhaps for many years past — three hundred and sixty-five times a year!

Yet one more:

I can never prevent myself from throwing a glance, if not sympathetic at least full of curiosity, over the crowd of outcasts who press around the enclosure of a public concert. From the orchestra, across the night, float songs of fête, of triumph, or of pleasure. The dresses of the women sweep and shimmer; glances pass; the well-to-do, tired with doing nothing, saunter about and make indolent pretence of listening to the music. Here are only the rich, the happy; here is nothing that does not inspire or exhale the pleasure of being alive, except the aspect of the mob that presses against the outer barrier yonder, catching gratis, at the will of the wind, a tatter of music, and watching the glittering furnace within.

There is a reflection of the joy of the rich deep in the eyes of the poor that is always interesting. But to-day, beyond this people dressed in blouses and calico, I saw one whose nobility was in striking contrast with all the surrounding triviality. She was a tall, majestic woman, and so imperious in all her air that I cannot remember having seen the like in the collections of the aristocratic beauties of the past. A perfume of exalted virtue emanated from all her being. Her face, sad and worn, was in perfect keeping with the deep mourning in which she was dressed. She also, like the plebeians she mingled with and did not see, looked upon the luminous world with a profound eye, and listened with a toss of her head.

It was a strange vision. "Most certainly," I said to myself, "this poverty, if poverty it be, ought not to admit of any sordid economy; so noble a face answers for that. Why then does she remain in surroundings with which she is so strikingly in contrast?"

But in curiously passing near her I was able to divine the reason. The tall widow held by the hand a child dressed like herself in black. Modest as was the price of entry, this price perhaps sufficed to pay for some of the needs of the little being, or even more, for a superfluity, a toy.

She will return on foot, dreaming and meditating — and alone, always alone, for the child is turbulent and selfish, without gentleness or patience, and cannot become, any more than another animal, a dog or a cat, the confidant of solitary griefs.

THE TEMPTATIONS; OR, EROS, PLUTUS, AND GLORY.

Last night two superb Satans and a She-devil not less extraordinary ascended the mysterious stairway by which Hell gains access to the frailty of sleeping man, and communes with him in secret. These three postured gloriously before me, as though they had been upon a stage — and a sulphurous splendour emanated from these beings who so disengaged themselves from the opaque heart of the night. They bore with them so proud a presence, and so full of mastery, that at first I took them for three of the true Gods.

The first Satan, by his face, was a creature of doubtful sex. The softness of an ancient Bacchus shone in the lines of his body. His beautiful languorous eyes, of a tenebrous and indefinite colour, were like violets still laden with the heavy tears of the storm; his slightly-parted lips were like heated censers, from whence exhaled the sweet savour of many perfumes; and each time he breathed, exotic insects drew, as they fluttered, strength from the ardours of his breath.

Twined about his tunic of purple stuff, in the manner of a cincture, was an iridescent Serpent with lifted head and eyes like embers turned sleepily towards him. Phials full of sinister fluids, alternating with shining knives and instruments of surgery, hung from this living girdle. He held in his right hand a flagon containing a luminous red fluid, and inscribed with a legend in these singular words:

"DRINK OF THIS MY BLOOD: A PERFECT
RESTORATIVE";

and in his left hand held a violin that without doubt served to sing his pleasures and pains, and to spread abroad the contagion of his folly upon the nights of the Sabbath.

From rings upon his delicate ankles trailed a broken chain of gold, and when the burden of this caused him to bend his eyes towards the earth, he would contemplate with vanity the nails of his feet, as brilliant and polished as well-wrought jewels.

He looked at me with eyes inconsolably heartbroken and giving forth an insidious intoxication, and cried in a chanting voice: " If thou wilt, if thou wilt, I will make thee an overlord of souls; thou shalt be master of living matter more perfectly than the sculptor is master of his clay; thou shalt taste the pleasure, reborn without end, of obliterating thyself in the self of another, and of luring other souls to lose themselves in thine."

But I replied to him: " I thank thee. I only gain from this venture, then, beings of no more worth than my poor self? Though remembrance brings me shame indeed, I would forget nothing; and even before I recognised thee, thou ancient monster, thy mysterious cutlery, thy equivocal phials, and the chain that imprisons thy feet, were symbols showing clearly enough the inconvenience of thy friendship. Keep thy gifts."

The second Satan had neither the air at once tragical and smiling, the lovely insinuating ways, nor the delicate and scented beauty of the first. A gigantic man, with a coarse, eyeless face, his heavy paunch overhung his hips and was gilded and pictured, like a tattooing, with a crowd of little moving figures which represented the unnumbered forms of universal misery. There were little sinew-shrunken men who hung themselves willingly from nails; there were meagre gnomes, deformed and under-sized, whose beseeching eyes begged an alms even more eloquently than their trembling hands; there were old mothers who nursed clinging abortions at their pendent breasts. And many others, even more surprising.

This heavy Satan beat with his fist upon his immense belly, from whence came a loud and resounding metallic clangour, which died away in a sighing made by many human voices. And he smiled unrestrainedly, showing his broken teeth — the imbecile smile of a man who has dined too freely. Then the creature said to me:

" I can give thee that which gets all, which is worth all, which takes the place of all." And he tapped his monstrous paunch, whence came a sonorous echo as the commentary to his obscene speech. I turned away with disgust and replied: "I need no man's misery to bring me happiness; nor will I have the sad wealth of all the misfortunes pictured upon thy skin as upon a tapestry."

As for the She-devil, I should lie if I denied that at first I found in her a certain strange charm, which to define I can but compare to the charm of certain beautiful women past their first youth, who yet seem to age no more, whose beauty keeps something of the penetrating magic of ruins. She had an air at once imperious and sordid, and her eyes, though heavy, held a certain power of fascination. I was struck most by her voice, wherein I found the remembrance of the most delicious *contralti*, as well as a little of the hoarseness of a throat continually laved with brandy.

" Wouldst thou know my power ? " said the charming and paradoxical voice of the false goddess. " Then listen." And she put to her mouth a gigantic trumpet, enribboned, like a *mirliton*, with the titles of all the newspapers in the world; and through this trumpet she cried my name so that it rolled through space with the sound of a hundred thousand thunders, and came re-echoing back to me from the farthest planet.

" Devil! " cried I, half tempted. " that at least is worth something." But it vaguely struck me, upon examining the seductive virago more attentively, that I had seen her clinking glasses with certain drolls of my acquaintance, and her blare of brass carried to my ears I know not what memory of a fanfare prostituted.

So I replied, with all disdain: " Get thee hence! I know better than wed the light o' love of them that I will not name."

Truly, I had the right to be proud of a so courageous renunciation. But unfortunately I awoke, and all my courage left me. " In truth," I said, " I must have been very deeply asleep indeed to have had such scruples. Ah, if they would but return while I am awake, I would not be so delicate."

So I invoked the three in a loud voice, offering to dishonour myself as often as necessary to obtain their favours; but I had without doubt too deeply offended them, for they have never returned.

THE END

Printed in the United States
29357LVS00006B/115